Citizen Participation and the
Urban Policy Process

Citizen Participation and the Urban Policy Process

Richard L. Cole
The George Washington University

Lexington Books
D.C. Heath and Company
Lexington, Massachusetts
Toronto   London

Library of Congress Cataloging in Publication Data

Cole, Richard L.
   Citizen participation and the urban policy process.

   Originally presented as the author's thesis, Purdue University, 1973.
   Bibliography: p.
   1. Municipal government—United States. 2. Decentralization in govern-
ment—United States. 3. Political participation—United States. I. Title.
JS341.C64 1974   352.073   73-18246
ISBN 0-669-91892-X

Published simultaneously in Canada.

Printed in the United States of America.

International Standard Book Number: 0-669-91892-X

Library of Congress Catalog Card Number: 73-18246

Contents

List of Figures

List of Tables

Preface

During the 1960s and early 1970s a number of municipalities, supported by various philosophical and political concerns and encouraged by federal-funding requirements, initiated a variety of programs of citizen participation. These programs have been variously labeled: multiple service centers, neighborhood councils, little city halls, city hall annexes, mini-governments, and so forth. All these programs are designed to provide the citizen with a more direct means of participating in the political affairs of the community.

The existence of these programs presents several interesting questions for the student of urban politics. These questions include: What social and political environments are most conducive to citizen participation? What is the effect of federal policy on urban decentralization? What are the attitudinal and demographic characteristics of those participating in these programs, and how do these characteristics compare with those of the neighborhood as a whole? What are the effects of participation on the participants' trust, efficacy, and perception of improved delivery of goods and services? And, what are the implications of these various findings for the future of citizen involvement? Answers to these questions have important theoretical implications and should provide a more rational basis for the evaluation of citizen participation as an alternative to the present urban situation.

In order to assess these concerns, data from several sources were employed. Included was a survey of decentralization efforts in all cities over 50,000; personal interviews and on-site inspections of several ongoing participation programs; interviews with a number of public officials; and various census and official governmental reports.

A participation index was constructed comprised of two of the most important dimensions of citizen involvement upon which all programs examined in this study were ranked. One of these dimensions measured the scope of program coverage, the other measured the intensity of actual control exercised by citizen participants.

Factor analysis was used to reduce a vast number of political and socioeconomic variables to the fewest important dimensions of the urban environment, and it was found that those factors representing population size, federal-funding support, race, mayor's voting power, and urban violence were the most important predictors of the citizen participation index. Based on this analysis, it was concluded that (1) there will be a reduction in the absolute number of citizen participation programs following the expiration of Model Cities and Office of Economic Opportunity (OEO) legislation; (2) these programs will not be totally abolished; (3) those programs remaining will average a lower score on the involvement index than that which is currently observed.

It was found that neither black nor white participants viewed their participation either as a step toward racial separation or as a means of political confrontation. Most reported simply a general interest in community improvement as their motive for participation. It was found that the socioeconomic characteristics of the participants were higher than those of their neighborhood as a whole and that this discrepancy ratio increased as the program's ranking on the participation index increased.

It was also found that most citizens were satisfied with the ability of their program to accomplish a more favorable allocation of goods and services to the neighborhood and that most reported an increase in political trust and confidence attitudes attributable to their participation. Most important, however, these relationships were found to be curvilinear. Those at the upper and lower ends of the program continuum were the *least* satisfied with the program's success and reported the *least* degree of improvement in political trust. It was suggested that an "optimum zone of program typology" can be identified which maximizes both goals of citizen satisfaction and improved political trust.

It was suggested that a program designed to achieve the goals of the participatory model of democracy can be judged successful to the extent to which it (1) positively affects the political efficacy and confidence of those involved; and (2) enlists and maintains the support of the average citizen. It was found that programs of citizen involvement in municipal politics can satisfy, to some extent, the first requirement but have not been able to accomplish the second goal.

It was suggested, in conclusion, that the most rational federal policy toward citizen participation is one which provides considerable discretion to individual communities in determining whether to adopt a program of citizen involvement, and the most rational policy for individual urban areas is one promoting programs avoiding the extreme forms of neighborhood control and large-scale decentralization efforts.

Acknowledgments

This research was assisted by a David Ross Grant awarded by the Purdue Research Foundation. For that grant, I am most grateful. A note of appreciation is due the Advisory Commission on Intergovernmental Relations and the International City Management for providing data which were invaluable to the completion of this research. Carl Stenberg, Senior Analyst of the Advisory Commission on Intergovernmental Relations provided valuable advice and assistance at a very crucial stage of the preparation of this manuscript.

I am indebted also to Professors Richard Haines, Myron Hale, and William Shaffer for their comments and suggestions at every stage of this research. Their suggestions greatly improved this manuscript. A special debt of gratitude is owed Professor David A. Caputo who has lent a considerable amount of time and talent to this project.

I am, also, grateful to Dotty Eberle for the outstanding execution of her typing and editorial skills which she cheerfully performed under considerable pressure.

Finally, this study would not have been possible were it not for the cooperation received from those private citizens and public officials who generously allowed themselves to be questioned, observed, and examined by still one more student of urban politics. To them, especially, I must express my sincerest appreciation.

Of course, none of these individuals is responsible for any errors or omissions in this manuscript.

**Citizen Participation and the
Urban Policy Process**

1
Introduction: Citizen Participation, Democratic Theory, and a Method of Classification

During the past decade demands for increased participation "in the decisions which affect them" have been common among such diverse (and sometimes antagonistic) groups as blacks, factory workers, consumers, students, and the poor. However, it is at the level of municipal politics (where some have said that such participation appeals both to "those who look forward to a time in American cities in which racial peace and amity will prevail and to those who dream of the day when municipal services again will successfully perform the function for which they are responsible"[1]) where the implementation of channels for direct participation have been most fully developed. In a recent study, Carl Stenberg found that almost two-thirds of all city officials responding to a mailed questionnaire reported some form of citizen participation activity in their municipality.[2] In another study, Joseph Zimmerman catalogued the wide variety of structures and forms which these programs have assumed. Examples of the programs include city hall annexes in Kansas City; a neighborhood center for social services in Santa Fe Springs, California; neighborhood service centers in San Antonio; store-front offices in San Diego; a hot line in Charlotte, North Carolina; complaint bureaus in Indianapolis, Houston, Los Angeles, Jacksonville, and New York City; community service officers in Savannah; town hall meetings in Norfolk; and neighborhood councils in Dayton, Boston, and Sacramento.[3] Clearly, the movement for direct citizen participation in local politics has assumed widely diverse structures and forms in a variety of cities.

This is a study which explores these various channels of participation in municipal politics and the conditions associated with each. However, the student of local politics is interested not only in the structural variety of citizen involvement programs and the socioeconomic and political environments which give rise to each; he is also interested in citizen participation because of its impact on the individual participant, the political system as a whole, and, ultimately, upon democratic theory and representative government. Thus these concerns: the environmental conditions associated with the various citizen participation programs, the implications of citizen participation for democratic theory and practice, and the consequences of such participation for the citizen and the system as a whole are the principle themes to be examined in this book. Although the initiation of many of these participation activities certainly did not originate from the citizens themselves, the programs have been supported by various philosophic, practical, and political concerns. This introductory chapter outlines the theoretical and philosophical foundations of the municipal citizen

1

participation movement; discusses the practical policy objectives of
involvement; reviews the political considerations involved; and develo
subsequent analysis, a classificatory scheme of citizen participation progra

Citizen Participation and Democratic Theory

Before it became public policy, citizen participation, like much social legis
was associated principally with the academic and intellectual comm
However, as Daniel Moynihan notes, citizen involvement differs from
social initiatives of this century in the speed with which it was trans:
"from university lecture room and professional Journals to the halls of C
and the statute books of the national government."[4] In fact, as a philos
idea, citizen participation is a product of two schools of academic thoug
sociological view concerned primarily with the effect of the loss of com
on society as a whole; and the political science view concerned mainly w
effects of nonparticipation on the individual's psychological and educ
development. Each of these perspectives is summarized below.

According to the sociological view (associated especially with such sch
Robert Nisbert, William Kornhauser, Eric Fromm, and Maurice Stei
distinguishing characteristic of postwar American society has been the ero
all those institutions such as the family, job, church, and especial
community through which individuals can relate to one another, form all
and take political initiatives. As Stein remarks, "Industrialization [
century has] ripped apart the fabric of community life. Meaning and p
had to be sought outside the factory, but the more personal sources—r
and the family—were also in the throes of change."[5] Nisbet, also, finds t
key conditions of contemporary American society are disorganization, d
insecurity, and instability.[6] As a consequence of such conditions and
absence of such buffers as the family, the church, and the community
"atomized" state as Kornhauser calls it[7]), people are more likely
influenced and mobilized by a totalitarian elite. According to Moynihan
need a sense of community. Having no other institution at hand, me
unavoidably turned to the state to provide this sense, and that has rep
and probably necessarily ended in totalitarianism."[8]

Likewise, Kornhauser is concerned with the future of stable democra
mass (i.e., lacking in primary institutions) society. The lack of contac
cohesion provided by groups such as the community leaves the individu
state of apathy and discontent, according to Kornhauser. People i
condition, he believes, are readily available for elite manipulation and m
tion. Group identification, according to Kornhauser, is the bulwark of l
Not only do such groups protect the elite from unnecessary pressure fr
masses, they protect the masses from illegitimate (totalitarian) manipulat
the elite.[9]

similar manner, Stein believes that the process of urbanization, industrial-
, and bureaucratization and, consequently, the loss of community ties
n to "shape the destinies of communities and individuals along irrevo-
ines. . . ." "We have," he says, "reached the results of that process within
ois society which, call it alienation with Marx or anomie with Durkheim,
rms the human being into an object." As a result, he believes, "com-
ties become increasingly dispensable. . . . *Individuals become increasingly
'ent upon centralized authorities and agencies in all areas of life.*"[10]
t which is being treated here as the sociological view of participation,
stresses the threat to democratic society of the erosion of primary,
-face, groups. Such an erosion, according to this view, leads to mass
·, alienation, loss of identification, and apathy. In such a condition, the
are susceptible to centralized and even totalitarian rule. The cure for such
tion, obviously, is seen by these scholars as the encouragement of more
channels of citizen involvement. Summarizing the recommendations of
of these theorists, Moynihan finds their cure to be, "the creation of new
tions, or the revival of old ones, which, given meaningful functions, would
lly acquire authority whereupon a multiplicity of authorities would come
istence in the interstices of which freedom could live."[11]
course there are areas of overlap and a considerable amount of similarity
n the sociological view and the political science perspective. However, to
ent greater than the sociologists, the political scientists of the 1960s and
advocating direct means of citizen participation are more concerned with
ychological effects of such participation (or nonparticipation) on the
ual. As Peter Bachrach, one of the leading proponents of this school of
al thought (sometimes called participatory democrats), states: "I believe
theory of democracy should be based upon the following assumptions and
les: the majority of individuals stand to gain in self-esteem and growth
l a fuller affirmation of their personalities by participating more actively
ningful community decisions. . . ."[12] Likewise, Jack Walker has argued
'by taking part in the affairs of his society the citizen should gain in
edge and understanding, develop a deeper sense of social responsibility,
oaden his perspectives beyond the narrow confines of his private life."[13]
se familiar with classical democratic theory may be puzzled with the
on that the advocacy of direct means of citizen involvement in public
by students of political thought (such as Bachrach and Walker) departs
vhat has become known as contemporary democratic theory.[14] Partici-
in public affairs is, after all, central to the writings of such celebrated
ratic philosophers as Rousseau, John Stuart Mill, and Bentham. Neverthe-
articipation has played a minimal role in contemporary political thought
s Carole Pateman argues, the emphasis of contemporary democratic
rs generally is placed "on the dangers inherent in wide popular partici-
in politics."[15]
s discrepancy between classical and contemporary democratic thought is

due largely to the attempt by contemporary students of political affairs to reconcile classical theories of how democracy should work with findings revealed by empirical investigations into political attitudes and behavior conducted since the Second World War. These surveys have found that, contrary to what is understood to be the classical notion of democratic man, most individuals are generally uninterested in politics, uninformed about political events, and perhaps worst of all display antidemocratic attitudes. In one of the earliest comprehensive studies of American voting patterns, the authors of *Voting* show that the behaviors and attitudes of those included in their survey fall far short of the democratic ideal at almost every instance. They demonstrate that a great number of people are lacking in political motivation, interest, and knowledge.[16] Despite these deficiencies, however, the authors conclude that the democratic system is not in jeopardy. They state: "Individual voters seem unable to satisfy the requirements for a democratic system of government outlined by [classical] political theorists. But the *system of democracy* does meet certain requirements for a going political organization. The individual members may not meet all the standards, but the whole nevertheless survives and grows."[17]

Unlike those political theorists who today are advocating a more direct role for the individual, Bernard Berelson and the other authors of *Voting* clearly deflate the role of the individual in democratic politics and emphasize instead the vitality of the system as a whole.[18] They go on to argue that low commitment to political causes and beliefs contribute to the stability of the system. As Pateman summarizes Berelson's thesis, "limited participation and apathy have a positive function for the whole system by cushioning the shock of disagreement, adjustment and change."[19]

Even prior to Berelson's (and others') demonstration of the failures of the citizen to meet the requirements of classical theory, Joseph Schumpeter had significantly altered democratic thought. Schumpeter's main criticism of earlier theorists was their emphasis on democracy as an *end* itself, rather than as a method for arriving at decisions.[20] Democracy, according to Schumpeter, should be defined as "that institutional arrangement for arriving at political decisions in which individuals acquire the power to decide by means of a competitive struggle for the peoples' vote."[21] The basic means for participation open to the citizen in Schumpeter's thesis is voting for leaders. Thus, according to Schumpeter's redefinition of democracy, there is almost no room for active participation by the individual, rather the focus is on competition for power among elites.

Other political scientists have added important dimensions to this contemporary theory of democracy. Most notable of these are Robert Dahl, Giovanni Sartori, and Raymond Aron.[22] However, the primary elements of postwar democratic theory, and especially the proposed role of the individual in democratic practice, are well illustrated in the writings of Schumpeter and Berelson. Above all, according to this view, democracy is seen as a representative process. The role of the average citizen is limited to selecting among competing elites those who should hold office. Moreover, the apathy and disinterest expressed by a large proportion of the electorate (as revealed in survey research) is viewed as functional for the system. High levels of participation are viewed as potentially dangerous since it is among the lower classes, who are generally the most apathetic, that authoritarian dispositions are most frequently found.[23] In summary, the emphasis in what has been called contemporary (as distinguished from classical or radical) democratic theory is placed on the stability and vitality of the *system* as a whole, rather than on the individual.

The classical theory of democracy (a version of which those labeled participatory democrats are today advocating) is, of course, quite different. Perhaps the outstanding characteristic of democracy as envisioned by those philosophers (and particularly when compared with the writings of Schumpeter, Dahl, and Berelson) was the role accorded individual participation in political affairs and especially the educational effects which such participation would have for the individual. As Bachrach notes in his review of classical democratic thought, "The emphasis in classical democratic theory upon citizen participation . . . is based upon the premise that such involvement is an essential means to the full development of individual capabilities."[24]

Direct participation by each citizen in the making of all political decisions was, of course, the underlying principle of Rousseau's political theory. Out of such a decision-making process (assuming, as Rousseau had hoped, that all participants would be roughly equal in economic resources) the general will of all participants was most likely to be adopted as policy. However, as Pateman clearly shows, participation of all citizens meant far more to Rousseau than simply insuring the will of a few would not dominate. Of major emphasis for Rousseau (as well as for other classical and today's radical democratic theorists) was the psychological benefits of participation for the individual. Pateman states, "Rousseau's ideal system is designed to develop responsible, individual social and political action through the effect of the participatory process."[25] John Stuart Mill also believed that one of the primary advantages of participatory government is its educative function. He argued, as Peter Eisinger points out, that the individual who is denied the right of participation in public affairs is limited in his capacity for responsible public action. The individual who participates in decision-making is forced, according to Mill, to "weigh interests not his own; to be guided, in the case of conflicting claims, by another rule than his private partialities; to apply at every turn, principles and maxims which have for their reason of existence the common good."[26] Interestingly, Mill also argued that it is at the local (rather than national) level that the individual is most likely to be able to effectively participate in public affairs. According to Pateman, "Thus, for Mill, it is at the local level where the real educative effect of participation occurs."[27]

Thus the classical model of the democratic process stresses direct partici-

pation of the individual in the decision-making process. Above all, it
psychological and educational benefits that accrue to the individual (rathe
the stability of the system) which is cherished by these political philosoph
Walker states, the classical theorists "were *not* primarily concerned wi
policies which might be produced in a democracy; above all else they
concerned with *human development*, the opportunities which existed in pe
activities to realize the untapped potentials of man. . . ."[28]

Since it is clear that those political scientists who today argue for inc
citizen involvement in municipal affairs (such as Bachrach, Walker, Henry
and T.B. Bottomore) are applying principles similar to those of cl
democratic thought, it is important to stress the difference between that
and the contemporary model, and it is especially important to understa
implications of each model for the individual citizen.

The principal concern of the participation model is the developmer
system designed to promote and enhance the potentials of the average ine
al. System stability is not so much a concern (although Pateman argue
there is no problem of instability in the participatory model since
self-sustaining through the educative impact of the participation process"
are the beneficial effects of participation upon the citizenry. Obvious
participation model envisions an active role for the individual, where
contemporary (sometimes called elitist) model focuses upon (even encov
the passivity of most individuals. The principal actors in the contem
model are competing elite and, from this perspective, the stability of the s
lies in the sense of responsibility of its elected leaders. Above a
participation model developed by political scientists stresses and encoura
active role for the individual. Summarizing the participation model, Pa
states, "One might characterize the participation model as one where ma
input (participation) is required and where output includes not just p
(decisions) but also the development of the social and political capabili
each individaul. . . ."[30]

These, then, summarize the theoretical and philosophical justificatio
vanced by many sociologists and political scientists who began in the 195
1960s to advocate increased participation in community affairs. The soci
is most concerned with the threat to democratic systems and the socia
posed by the loss of face-to-face contacts, the political scientist is
concerned with the debilitating effects which nonparticipation has on the
and psychological development of the individual. These problems co
corrected, each school has argued, by pursuing policies which would p
more opportunities for direct participation in community affairs. As Mo
found, "during the 1960's, in particular, they [social and political scie
have had quite extraordinary access to power. And they have used this ac
considerable measure to promote social change [participation] in directio
deem necessary and desirable. In particular, they would appear to have bu

thy with the desire for order. . . . The reaction among many [active social
sts] was not to be appalled by disorder, *but almost to welcome it.*"[31]   It
be clear, also, that within both disciplines this advocacy of direct
pation has touched off heated and prolonged debates between those who
prefer a less direct role and those preferring a more meaningful
pation role for the individual.[32]
wever (and with deference to Moynihan's emphasis on the academic and
ctual pressures for citizen involvement), it probably is fair to conclude
he movement for greater citizen participation in local politics has not
ped to the extent it has today solely on the basis of academic appeals nor
kely that the future of citizen participation is totally dependent on who
or who loses these scholarly debates. Rather, citizen participation as it
ped in the 1960s had strong *practical* and, for a time, *political* support as
articularly strong advocates of increased citizen involvement have been
ity, often black, urban residents as well as a number of public (state,
and federal) officials. Furthermore, these more practical justifications for
pation are, at least in the short run, more testable than those philosophical
ns reviewed above. The following section discusses the movement for
participation from the more pragmatic perspectives of urban residents
blic administrators.

Participation, Urban
ers, and the Delivery
nicipal Services

e variety of practical justifications for increasing channels of neighborhood
pation in municipal affairs have been advanced. Such involvement, some
aggested, will increase the quality of services to the neighborhood, increase
s' feelings of political efficacy, increase administrative attentiveness to
orhood needs, develop neighborhood leadership, and promote community
on.[33] However, the vast majority of these justifications, as will be
ented below, can be classified into two groups: those which would suggest
uch participation will lead to better, or at least more accountable,
pal services at the neighborhood level; and those which would argue that
involvement will increase citizen trust and confidence in public officials,
educing the likelihood of urban unrest and violence. These views are
ively classified as the neighborhood (or citizen) perspective and the
istrative (or official) perspective. From the perspective of neighborhood
inority leaders, citizen participation offers the possibility of a more
ble distribution of municipal goods and services; from the perspective of
ban administrator, such participation offers the possibility of reduced
tensions. Commenting on these two interpretations, Katznelson finds that

the term *citizen participation* "can be seen to mask two wholly different political responses. The 'subordinates' [neighborhood] view which seeks new structural relations . . . and the 'rulers' [official] view which sees decentralization as a relatively costless device to link disaffected citizens to the polity."[34]

It is because of these differing, and sometimes conflicting, expectations of citizen participation programs that the study of citizen involvement offers such an interesting challenge to the policy analyst. It might be found that a program designed to have a maximum positive effect on the participants' trust and confidence in local officials may have the opposite effect on citizens' perceptions of the improved delivery of goods and services. Alternatively, it might be discovered that an optimum program structure exists which maximizes values of both citizens and officials. A classification scheme, which will allow evaluations of this sort to be attempted, is developed later in this chapter. This section more fully explores the differing policy objectives of neighborhood residents and municipal administrators.

Not only do the objectives of those who support various types of citizen participation structures sometimes differ, the advocacy of citizen involvement presents basic value dilemmas even to those who are *united* in their goal expectations of citizen participation programs. Urban officials, administrators, and many urban scholars for the past several decades have advocated a long list of reforms—including centralization of authority, reduction of the number of governmental units, and at-large elections—all designed to promote the values of economy, efficiency, and professionalism.[35] The movement for citizen participation in policy matters appears to be in direct contrast to these long-standing proposals. Nevertheless, an increasing number of urban administrators have been willing to abandon these traditional values and to accept, to some degree, increased citizen involvement.

This changing attitude on the part of urban administrators is vividly reflected in three documents published in the late 1960s. In 1967 the Advisory Commission on Intergovernmental Relations recommended that large cities be allowed to establish neighborhood subunits of government with elected neighborhood councils. These councils would be responsible for providing various services in the neighborhoods and would have the authority to levy taxes.[36] In 1968 the National Commission on Urban Problems recommended to the Congress and the president that "large city governments take prompt and affirmative steps to decentralize appropriate municipal services to the neighborhood level, and to establish channels of communication with neighborhood residents."[37] Likewise, the 1968 National Advisory Commission on Civil Disorder (Kerner Commission) endorsed the proposal that "city governments need new and more vital channels of communications to the residents of the ghetto; they need to improve their capacity to respond effectively to community needs before they become community grievances; and they need to provide opportunity for meaningful involvement of ghetto residents in shaping policies and programs which affect the community."[38]

This changing attitude of administrators and scholars coincides chronologically with the rising levels of urban tensions and violence in the late 1960s and reflects, to a large measure, the expectation of urban administrators that citizen involvement will reduce alienation and distrust. As one observer has commented, it is hoped by some officials that citizen participation will foster among citizens a "commitment to peaceful resolution of conflict, the absence of feelings of alienation, and a willingness to compromise."[39] W.G. Brooks has commented that it was expected by a few administrators and officials that citizen involvement programs would build "cadres of anti-rioters."[40] Numerous others have made essentially this same observation. Explaining the motives underlying citizen participation requirements in the federally funded urban renewal programs, Duby states, "Citizen participation was sought in order to avoid, or at least handle, protests that arose among the residents of the areas scheduled for renewal. In other words . . . programs for resident participation were often used to offset the spontaneous but disruptive activities of local protest groups."[41] In a similar vein, James Q. Wilson finds that citizen participation programs are widely regarded by urban mayors as a "means of ending the political alienation of . . . citizens."[42] A recent bulletin of the Advisory Commission on Intergovernmental Relations states that "decentralization has been proposed as one remedy to the alienation and isolation of life in the big cities."[43] In an excellent critique of the advantages and disadvantages of citizen involvement, David Hart concludes that "the main reason the advocates call for a totally participating society is due to their concern with . . . conflict behavior. While they are primarily concerned with individuals, they believe, nevertheless, that such behaviors are destructive to society. . . ."[44] As a final example, Joseph Zimmerman has argued that citizen participation must be justified on *noneconomic* grounds. Rather, the major objective of such programs, he believes, is that they should result "in a lowering of tensions between citizens and bureaucrats."[45] Thus the urban administrator has been willing to abandon his long-standing commitment to programs fostering such values as economy, efficiency, and professionalism and to adopt, at least temporarily, one which it is hoped will promote increased citizen trust and confidence in the political structure and will, therefore, reduce the incidents of urban unrest and violence.[46]

On the other hand, neighborhood leaders—especially black, ghetto residents—also have abandoned long-standing policy objectives in their advocacy of citizen participation programs. Many neighborhood leaders have for years assumed that the improvement of the urban condition could best be achieved through policies of cooperation and integration. Indeed, a number of studies (such as the influential *Coleman Report*) have indicated that, at least in the area of education, improvement is best achieved by the exposure of minority and disadvantaged students to integrated classroom situations. However, their inability to achieve satisfactory results has encouraged many of these same groups to seek some form of direct citizen influence in the decision-making process, including neighborhood control of public facilities. In 1970, for example, the

Congress of Racial Equality abandoned its goal of school integratic
adopted a plan incorporating the neighborhood school concept.[47] Unc
centralized conditions of local government which proponents of citizen i
ment oppose, argues Henry Schmandt, "minorities and the poor general
access to and a means of intervening in the administrative process
consequently are unable to make effective demands on the service delive
reward allocating structures. Disaggregation of authority to submunicipa
is viewed as a way of making the system more amenable to citizen influen
Likewise, Ralph Kramer defines this orientation as one which holds that
disadvantaged neighborhoods acquire political influence "can they char
community policies and conditions that prevent them from acquiring th
share of society's goods and services."[49]

From the perspective of disadvantaged neighborhood groups, then,
participation is urged as a method for obtaining a more equitable share
allocation of municipal goods and services. As Wilson has noted,
neighborhood associations attempt to extract concessions [from mayc
matters of city policy (such as street sweeping, garbage collection, or play
maintenance) which affect their area."[50] Likewise, summarizing the pr
cons of decentralization, Yates finds the argument that citizen participati
"increase administrative attentiveness and responsiveness to neighbc
needs" a primary motive in the quest by neighborhood groups for inc
involvement.[51]

Thus, for varying reasons, urban scholars, administrators, and neighbc
leaders have been willing to abandon traditional social and administrative
and adopt instead proposals of citizen participation. Urban administrat
primarily interested in citizen involvement as a means of reducing levels o1
tension, neighborhood and minority leaders are hopeful that such partic
will result in a more favorable distribution of goods and services. George V
summarizes this dual objective of citizen participation programs when he
that citizen involvement must "improve the image of government but i
also improve services."[52]

One of the primary themes of the present study is that, despite the ex
number and variety of citizen participation programs which have been a
in the past ten years, no study is available which attempts to system:
determine how effective these programs are in achieving either or both c
objectives. Reviewing what he considers to be the "most important book
treatises on the subject" of citizen participation, Eisinger finds that the a
"neither possess nor can cite much hard evidence to support the various
they make."[53] Likewise in his summary of the citizen participation lite
Yates admits, "The key point about this debate, however, is that we have
no idea what the impact of decentralization actually is on an urban ne
hood. . . . There has been little empirical research on the impacts of e
decentralization experiences."[54] A primary purpose of this study, ther
present such an analysis.

 Participation, Political
t, and Federal-Funding
ements

ar it has been suggested that the movement for the direct involvement of
orhood residents in the political affairs of the community had strong
ic and practical support as it developed in the late 1960s. It is also true
e participation movement was encouraged by influential political support
quirements established by federal grants-in-aid programs as well. This
 reviews this political support and focuses especially on the impact of
 grant requirements on local citizen participation activities.

an extent far surpassing programs of previous years, many of the federal
to-local-governments programs of the 1960s required a considerable
 of neighborhood participation in the planning and execution of those
s. The three most important of these programs—Urban Renewal, the
nic Opportunity Act, and Model Cities—are discussed below. Here it is
the strong political support which President Johnson initially lent to these
ns and especially to the Economic Opportunity Act. Assuming the
ncy from Kennedy in 1963, it is reported that Johnson immediately
ed and endorsed Kennedy's antipoverty proposal which was under the
stration's consideration at the time of the assassination. The proposal
passed as the Economic Opportunity Act of 1964) encouraged (even
d) a maximum degree of neighborhood participation in the program's
ion. Johnson's motives for acceptance of the proposal are somewhat
e. Some have argued that Johnson was attracted to the measure because
deep concern with the predicament of the poor. According to Walter
Johnson's comment when first briefed on the program (just two days
king office) was, "That's my kind of program. It will help people. I want
 move full speed ahead on it."[55] Others have suggested that, regardless of
n's personal feelings, the poverty legislation became his test of leadership
ssuming office. According to Moynihan, "for the Johnson men it [the
 program] was a measure of their own President's ability to take hold
d. All concerned wanted to see results."[56]
any case, it is clear that the antipoverty program, which was to
antly affect neighborhood participation in local affairs, received President
n's unequivocal support. In fact, as reported by many, the president
 the measure as the essence of *his* Great Society program. With excerpts
ohnson's first State of the Union address, William Selover comments:

administration," he told a joint session of Congress on January 8, 1964,
 here and now declares unconditional war on poverty in America. . . ." He
t say, "this country" or "this government" but specifically "this
stration," and he distinctly did not ask "this congress" to declare war. . . .
hnson was intent on making this program uniquely his—the cornerstone of
at Society.[57]

Also, Sar Levitan finds that not only was Johnson personally committed to the legislation but that his support of the bill was instrumental in its passage. Levitan states, "The fact that the antipoverty bill passed through Congress relatively unscathed was not due to a general consensus in favor of the program. When the final vote was taken, Congress was still divided. Had it not been for the sustained pressure by President Johnson generating wide public support for the legislation, . . . the bill might have failed."[58]

There was additional political support for the 1964 antipoverty program. In particular, notes Levitan, a number of large city mayors were pressuring for quick passage in anticipation of the availability of large sums of poverty funds.[59] Nevertheless, it is clear that the primary political support of this measure—which was to so drastically alter the nature of citizen participation—was President Johnson. As will be discussed below, despite his support, it is relatively certain that Johnson (nor anyone else connected with the program at this stage) was fully aware of its implications for neighborhood participation. Yet Alan Altshuler was to comment in 1970 that "the whole current movement for neighborhood control was largely set in motion by the Economic Opportunity Act of 1964."[60]

However, as mentioned above, the Economic Opportunity Act of 1964 was only one of a series of federal programs having an influence on community participation. In addition to this program, two others—Urban Renewal and Model Cities—are also important. These three, and the significance of each for the participation movement, are discussed in detail below.

The Urban Renewal Program (as established by the Housing Act of 1954) is significant because it is the first major piece of federal legislation requiring citizen input. As David Ranney states, "The new concept [citizen input] was a response to criticism from proponents of housing legislation who claimed that urban redevelopment had resulted in an inhumane bulldozer approach to urban problems."[61] Thus the Housing Act of 1954 established seven new guidelines (known as the "workable program") which had to be met as a condition of receiving federal funds, one of which was a "program of citizen participation in the planning and execution of the project."[62] For the most part, committees formed in accordance with this requirement have been blue-ribbon panels, appointed by the mayor or planning staff and largely ignoring input from residents of the project area. In his review of federal programs, Melvin Mogulof labels participation in urban renewal as largely elitist.[63] Likewise, in her construction of a "ladder of citizen participation," Sherry Arnstein uses Urban Renewal as a prime example of the bottom rung of the ladder, that which she calls "manipulation."[64]

Recently, the Department of Housing and Urban Development has required more direct citizen input in its Urban Renewal program and in 1969 required the establishment of Project Area Committees comprised of residents of the project area in which residential rehabilitation activites are contemplated.[65] To some, this new requirement promises a shift in emphasis toward more meaningful resident input; however Urban Renewal is still firmly controlled by elected officials and remains an outstanding example of limited resident input and maximum retention by officials of decision-making responsibility.[66] For the purposes of this study, Urban Renewal is significant because it was the first in a series of federally funded programs requiring citizen input in the dispersion of those funds.

As previously mentioned, the establishment of the Community Action Program (CAP) by the Economic Opportunity Act of 1964 profoundly altered the federal government's attitude toward citizen participation. Although it appears that few were aware of its complete implications when passed,[67] the 1964 act did call for the "maximum feasible participation of residents of the area and members of the group served."

In light of later experiences, it is especially interesting that few in President Johnson's administration or in the Congress realized at the time the impact which the maximum feasible participation phrase would have on community participation. In his detailed discussion of events leading to the passage of the Economic Opportunity Act, Levitan writes that administration officials who critiqued the first drafts of the bill "neither questioned nor commented upon this phrase [the maximum feasible participation clause]. Nor was it considered significant enough to be mentioned in the official summary of the bill which was released, as is customary, when the bill was submitted to Congress."[68] Levitan further argues that participation of the poor was originally intended only as a means to prevent local communities from discrimination, in the administration of the legislation, against minority groups. He states, "To most of the task force participants, 'maximum feasible participation' represented a nice sentiment and a means of giving the administrator of the program power to prevent segregation in community action programs."[69] Moynihan shares the view that the participation clause was intended only as a means to prevent racial discrimination in the program's execution. Discussing the concerns of the administration's task force which drew up the proposed bill, Moynihan states, "In as much as the local white power structure would control the allocation of community action money, how could it be ensured that impoverished Negroes would get something like a proportionate share? A simple idea accrued to someone present: why not include language that would require the poor to participate. Then, later, if in a given locale it became clear that Negroes were not sharing—that is, participating—in the benefits of the new program, Washington could intervene on grounds that requirements of the legislation were not being met."[70] The solution, according to Moynihan, was the inclusion of the phrase requiring maximum feasible participation.

Also in Congress the maximum participation clause received little attention. Although Levitan notes that the Congress made several substantive and administrative changes in the bill he concludes that the participation aspects were hardly debated. Levitan states that "the issue of participation by the poor in community action programs was completely ignored [by the Congress]."[71]

Thus, according to both these views of the origins of the Office of Economic Opportunity (OEO) legislation, the maximum participation phrase—which was to significantly alter the substance and style of neighborhood participation—was largely ignored by Congress and included by the Johnson administration only as a legal effort to prevent discrimination in the program's administration. Moynihan goes on to suggest that the phrase only became important when interpreted by OEO staff members (who, claims Moynihan, wished to "arouse" the poor, not help them) to require a tripartite arrangement—input by local businessmen, the local government, and the poor.[72]

In any case, this act and its subsequent amendments drastically affected the nature of neighborhood and community involvement. Commenting on this program, Mogulof states that OEO moved beyond coalition politics into the area of citizen control of decision-making processes.[73]

As is well documented,[74] the controversial Community Action Agencies assumed widely diverse roles in the over 800 communities in which they were established. In a few areas, mayors and local officials succeeded in maintaining tight control over their activities.[75] However, in other areas, CAAs were able to establish a considerable degree of autonomy. Arnstein, as mentioned above, has constructed a seven-rung ladder of citizen involvement (to be discussed more fully below) upon which she attempts to classify citizen participation programs. Significantly, she cites examples of CAAs functioning at almost every rung.[76] Although the ultimate impact of the Community Action program on urban society still is unclear, it is fair to conclude, as has one observer, that to an extent unparalleled in the history of federal sponsorship of local policy, this program did "promote the mobilization of the political power of the poor and the articulation of dissatisfaction at the grass-roots level, led to confrontation politics, . . . and increased the demand for effective citizen participation in governmental programs and community control of those programs."[77]

The third major federal program having an impact on community participation is the Model Cities program as established by the Demonstration Cities and Metropolitan Development Act of 1966. The purpose of this legislation is the "mobilization of public and private resources in a comprehensive and coordinated effort to solve the economic, physical, and social problems of blighted neighborhoods."[78] Although much broader in scope, Model Cities legislation in many ways represented a retreat from the extent of citizen participation achieved in some CAP programs. Unlike OEO requirements, all federal Model Cities funds are channeled directly to the municipal government, not to local organizations. In addition, Model Cities legislation contains no specific requirements concerning either the proportion or manner of selection of citizen representatives. Indeed, in his study of federally sponsored citizen participation legislation, Mogulof concludes that "the model cities legislation, with its great emphasis on the role of the city [government] might . . . be interpreted as a legislative reaction to the style and degree of citizen involvement in the Community Action Program effort."[79]

This review of the Urban Renewal, OEO, and Model Cities programs was necessary not only because of the tremendous impact which the three programs have had upon programs of community involvement but also because they illustrate the boundaries of conceptual and policy alternative concerns within which a policy analysis of citizen participation may be structured. At the conceptual level, these programs suggest an analytical scheme for the classification of citizen participation programs. Such programs may vary as to the intensity of citizen influence and scope of activity. *Intensity* of citizen influence refers to the degree of actual influence over program formation and execution exercised by citizens. In her previously mentioned study, Arnstein defines this dimension simply as "the extent of citizens' power in determining the end product."[80] Concerning the three federally sponsored programs reviewed above, Urban Renewal represents the least intense program of citizen involvement, OEO represents the most. *Scope* of activity refers to the number and variety of programs within the jurisdiction of a particular program. The scope of a neighborhood health clinic, for example, is more limited than that of a multiservice center which engages in several activities.[81] Concerning scope of activity, Urban Renewal represents the most focused program and Model Cities represents the potentially broadest.[82] Such a scheme is central to the analysis herein presented and is developed more fully in the following section.

At the policy-making level, these three programs illustrate the continuing debate over the degree and substance of citizen influence. The basic policy question remains one of whether citizen involvement should remain elitist and limited to advice and consultation such as manifest in Urban Renewal programs, or should citizen participation approach shared, mass power and even neighborhood control as achieved in some OEO programs. Underlying this policy dilemma are the more central questions of purpose of citizen involvement. Is such participation intended to secure a more favorable allocation of goods and services for neighborhood groups, or is citizen involvement intended to increase the trust and confidence of alienated individuals? Just as important is the issue of goal compatibility. Would the achievement of one goal (such as increased confidence) measurably hinder or reinforce the achievement of another (better services)? Assuming that answers to these questions of purpose and objectives vary from urban area to area and group to group, the policy analyst is interested in the determination of which participation experiences most effectively accomplish which objectives. These questions are considered in the body of this study (especially in Chapters 5 and 6). Those evaluation attempts which are available are discussed in the following section.

Limitations of Current Policy
Evaluation Attempts and a Method
of Classification

These, then, were the forces influencing the movement for citizen participation in community affairs. For some time, the intellectual and academic community had favored the establishment of more direct means of citizen involvement in public affairs. By the 1960s, as Moynihan notes, a number of these scholars held influential positions within the Kennedy and Johnson administrations' advisory staff. The movement also had the support of civil rights groups who had become increasingly dissatisfied and disappointed in the results achieved through previous tactics, and of local officials who feared continued levels of urban unrest and violence. Finally, the movement was (at least initially) strongly supported by the efforts of President Johnson and heavily influenced by federal grants-in-aid requirements. Responding to these pressures and incentives, almost two-thirds of all United States cities reported some form of citizen participation program, as mentioned in the opening paragraph of this chapter. This section reviews and critiques currently available attempts at evaluation of citizen participation policies and constructs a classification scheme to be used in subsequent chapters for program analysis.

Although much of the citizen participation literature is descriptive only, scattered attempts at program and policy evaluation are available. Milton Kotler, for example, presents an in-depth analysis of a small OEO-funded organization in Columbus, Ohio which he finds relatively successful in its attempt to secure a degree of local autonomy and control. This program, in fact, becomes Kotler's model for his prescription of political activity which other neighborhoods should pursue.[83] Mario Fantini and his associates present an extensive analysis of school decentralization in New York City.[84] Like Kotler's work, the Fantini study obviously suffers from its lack of comparability. In 1966 Brandeis University conducted a study of twenty OEO programs which, although largely descriptive, did attempt a comparative evaluation of the "extent and quality of participation and the effects of differences in participation on the policies and programs of the Community Action Agency."[85] Also available is an analysis by George Washnis of decentralization practices in twelve large urban areas.[86] These and other attempts at policy evaluation will be discussed more fully below. The purpose here is to illustrate that, although these studies have all been prepared by exceptionally qualified scholars, collectively and individually they illustrate the two crucial deficiencies of currently available attempts to evaluate the effectiveness of citizen participation activities. These deficiencies are: (1) the lack of an acceptable scheme of categorization; and (2) the lack of empirical data upon which success or failure may be determined.

The first step in policy analysis is the development of a classification scheme by which the policy as adopted and administered in differing areas may be categorized (such as per capita dollars spent for highways, hospitals, education, etc.) and compared. However, in attempting to categorize citizen participation programs, much of the earlier literature, including those mentioned above, treated citizen involvement in a nominal fashion only. That is, many students, in their discussion of the conditions associated with citizen participation programs and the impact of citizen influence, presented their arguments as though the alternatives were either the acceptance or rejectance of a plan for citizen participation.[87] In fact, as argued above, there are significant gradations of citizen influence. More recent scholars have recognized these differences and, in their analyses, many develop a typology based upon a single dimension continuum ranging from those programs in which citizen involvement is least intense (as the term was defined above) to those in which citizens exercise substantial or even total control. Mogulof, for example, states that there appears to be a scale-like quality to patterns of participation ranging from greater to less citizen control,[88] and Altshuler suggests that "community control should be conceived as a continuum rather than as an absolute."[89] Attempting to delineate the structural elements which would be included in the construction of such a scale, Douglas Yates suggests seven items of activity ("ordered in terms of increasing local autonomy and power"). These include: (1) stationing officials in localities; (2) seeking out opinions of local people; (3) making local people administrative agents; (4) making neighborhood administrators accountable to local citizens; (5) establishing elected officials at the local level; (6) giving localities control over policy and programs; and (7) giving localities control over fiscal resources. According to Yates, "these seven elements constitute one dimension along which decentralization can be defined."[90] Another widely cited scheme of participation intensity, as previously introduced, is the "ladder of citizen participation" developed by Sherry Arnstein. According to her scheme, citizen participation can be conceived in terms of eight rungs of a ladder, also ranging from least to most citizen influence. Her classification is schematically presented in Figure 1-1.

Although these scales (and others of similar unidimensional construction[91]) are more appropriate than the earlier nominal classifications and do seem to better capture the essential elements of decentralization programs, they fail to adequately permit intra- or inter-city comparisons. This is so for two very basic reasons: they fail to discriminate between the number and variety of programs which cities have initiated, and they fail to account for the scope of activities in which particular programs may be engaged. For example, using Yates's or Arnstein's scheme, one would assign the same scale value to a headstart program concerned with the single issue of pre-school education as to a multiservice center involved with a community's health, recreation, housing, and employment concerns, assuming each program displayed the same intensity of citizen influence. Likewise, again assuming intensity of participation to be equal, these scales would assign the same values to a city engaged in one urban renewal

Intensity of Citizen Participation

More

Citizen Control

Delegated Power

Partnership

Placation

Consultation

Informing

Therapy

Manipulation

Less

Figure 1-1. Eight Rungs on the Ladder of Citizen Participation. Source: Sherry R. Arnstein, "Eight Rungs on the Ladder of Citizen Participation," in Edgar S. Cahn and Barry A. Passett, eds., *Citizen Participation: Effecting Community Change* (New York: Praeger, 1971), p. 70.

program in which citizen participation was encouraged as to a city involved in several OEO, Model Cities, and Urban Renewal programs.

Thus it appears that the intensity scale used by some to compare citizen participation programs (which is, itself, an improvement over earlier, nominal classifications) could be made even more analytically useful by simply adding the dimensions of scope and variety. Yates commented: "A second dimension that should be considered is the number of program functions involved in different decentralization experiments."[92] If such a dimension were added, intra- and inter-city comparisons could be facilitated by assigning values to programs according to the following two-dimensioned matrix as illustrated in Figure 1-2.

Such a matrix, it should be noted, does not destroy the intensity factor which others have found to be significant. However, it does add to this factor an extra dimension which makes both intra- and inter-city comparisons more meaningful.[93]

The second major deficiency in the literature attempting to analyze and evaluate programs of citizen participation is the lack of empirical data upon which sound conclusions (rather than speculations) may be based. Eisinger was

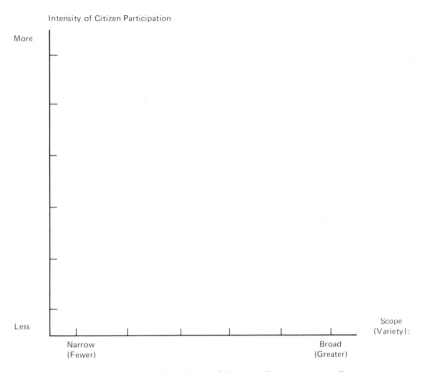

Figure 1-2. A Proposed Paradigm of Citizen Participation Programs.

quoted above as finding that the most important book-length treatments of citizen involvement programs neither possess nor can cite much empirical evidence to support their claims. Also commenting on the lack of information which would facilitate program evaluation, Mogulof states that "until the local vantage point is incorporated, it is clear that any policy recommendations must be based on speculations not grounded in the crucial dimension of live locally based experiences."[94] Speaking of the "sparseness of empirical date," Henry Schmandt finds that "a substantial portion of [the citizen participation literature] is normative in nature. Little is known about what types and degrees of urban decentralization will work and under what circumstances. As yet little is available in the way of systematic analysis or evaluation."[95] Likewise, Carl Stenberg notes the lack of criteria upon which evaluations of good or bad citizen participation programs might be evaluated."[96] As a final example, Howard Hallman has observed that, "as to the efficiency and program effectiveness of [programs of citizen involvement,] the results are not in as yet. . . ."[97]

The few attempts at comparative analysis which are available suffer either from examining too few programs to allow meaningful generalizations or from a neglect of collecting data so as to facilitate comparisons with other programs.

Paul Peterson, for example, has conducted an excellent study of three programs in Chicago, Philadelphia, and New York.[98] Although his study provides significant insights and interesting hypotheses for future research, Peterson's conclusions obviously are limited by his few case studies and the unique characteristics of the programs studied. One survey which did incorporate a relatively large sample size was the previously mentioned Brandeis study of twenty CAP programs.[99] However, this study focused primarily on descriptive aspects of each program (relationships of city size, percentage of blacks, government structure, and so forth to patterns of participation). Thus the otherwise instructive Brandeis study has very little to offer concerning the impact of citizen participation programs either on the level of municipal services or citizen alienation. One study which did attempt to gauge the impact of citizen participation was the recent survey conducted by the Advisory Commission on Intergovernmental Relations of city officials in all United States cities over 25,000.[100] However this study, by design, dealt exclusively with official attitudes and totally neglects opinions and attitudes of citizen representatives. Since, as documented above, two of the major objectives of citizen participation programs are the improvement of the delivery of goods and services *from the perspective of the neighborhood resident* and the improvement of *citizens'* images of government, it is mandatory that the opinions of citizen participants be incorporated in a complete policy evaluation of program results.

Summary: Citizen Participation
from a Policy Perspective

This chapter has reviewed the intellectual, political, and pragmatic forces influencing the movement for increased opportunities of citizen participation in municipal affairs. In response to these demands, it has been found, almost two-thirds of all American cities (over 25,000) have now adopted a program of citizen involvement. This chapter also reviewed the most important attempts to analyze and evaluate these programs. A number of crucial deficiencies in this literature were noted, including the lack of a satisfactory scheme of policy classification, the neglect of citizen attitudes and opinions, and most basic of all, simply the lack of comparable information (most available research is of the case-study variety). All of these studies have advanced interesting hypotheses concerning the environmental correlates and system-impacts of these programs, and these hypotheses are certainly not neglected in the analytical chapters which follow. However, because of their shortcomings, conclusive answers to the most important policy questions concerning citizen involvement cannot be answered by those studies presently available.

The present study, then, attempts to present a policy analysis of citizen participation programs in American cities which remedies to a significant degree the basic deficiencies discussed above. Specifically, this study differs from previous policy evaluation attempts in three fundamental areas. It is, first of all, comparative in nature. Data employed in the following analysis were collected from a wide variety of programs operating in several states (a complete description of the data is presented in the following chapter). Secondly, the analysis utilizes the conceptual scheme for program classification developed above. Central to that scheme, it will be recalled, is the assumption that citizen participation activities can best be described in terms of gradations of intensity of citizen involvement and scope of program coverage. Together these dimensions provide a two-dimensioned matrix of program scope and intensity upon which all programs may be measured and evaluated. Thus meaningful comparisons of both an inter- and intra-city nature are facilitated. Finally, the study relies heavily for its information upon the experiences of the citizens who have participated in these programs. Clearly, the most important actor in citizen participation programs is the citizen, and this study proceeds upon the assumption that, regardless of whether program objectives are defined in terms of improvement of services or improvement of the government's image, success or failure can best be measured from the perspective of the citizen participant.

In its organization, this study closely follows the familiar policy-process presentation. The policy-process model (described in more detail in Chapter 3) is particularly suited for providing answers to the types of questions about citizen participation for which there is at present only scattered and incomplete evidence. As will be discussed in Chapters 3 and 4, a number of those studies reviewed above have speculated upon the influence of local officials, the impact of federal encouragement (and requirements), the effect of urban violence, and the general social and economic conditions associated with the various programs. Through the application of the policy-process model, a reasonably accurate assessment of the individual and combined impacts of each of these environmental and political influences on citizen participation can be produced.

Also, as will be discussed below (Chapters 5 and 6), the impact or outcome of citizen participation programs on individual participants and on the system as a whole is the subject of a great deal of speculation and controversy. Application of the process model, with its emphasis on policy outcomes, will provide a much better estimation of the impact of citizen involvement programs than is presently available.

In addition, the analysis of citizen participation—a nonfiscal measure of policy output—should provide significant insights into the process of municipal policy-making itself. This is especially true since so many of the policy studies currently available (particularly at the urban level) employ only fiscal measures of public policy. The implications of this are discussed more fully in Chapters 3 and 4. The following chapter describes in detail the nature of the data collected for this study and the basic methodological assumptions and data-organization techniques to be employed throughout the analysis.

2

Citizen Participation in American Communities: An Analytical Scheme

In order that the substantive chapters of this study not be overly burdened or distracted with lengthy discussions of the methods of data collection, the interview processes, and the procedures of index and scale construction, this brief chapter is devoted to a presentation of this information. This is an important chapter for the analysis which follows since a large portion of the data used and many of the scales constructed are unique to this study. One of the most crucial limitations of the available literature, as discussed in Chapter 1, is its lack of comparability. That is, most research which has been conducted is of the case-study variety. Although that approach is useful as a guide for subsequent research, students of citizen participation in urban affairs currently have little information permitting meaningful generalizations or comparisons.

The data used in this analysis depart from that used in previous studies in that these have been collected from a wide variety of areas and program types. One source of data heavily relied upon is a 1970 questionnaire study conducted by the Advisory Commission on Intergovernmental Relations (ACIR) of participation activities in all United States cities over 25,000.[1] This study allows the ranking of the various programs according to an index of participation intensity and variety (described below) and thus the determination of the environmental and political correlates of the various program types. A second source of data is an in-depth survey, conducted specifically for this study, of the characteristics, attitudes, motives, and opinions of citizens participating in a variety of programs.[2] Each of these surveys, as well as other sources of data, is described more fully below.

Citizen Participation Activities and Indices of the Urban Environment

The policy-process model, as discussed above, is concerned with the environmental and political correlates of the policy under consideration. In order to estimate these influences, it is of course necessary that the researcher possess measures of the policy as well as important aspects of the political and social environment. The specific hypotheses to be examined by this phase of the model are discussed and tested in Chapters 3 and 4. Here, an index of citizen participation in American cities is constructed and the various indices of the urban political and social environment, unique to this study, are discussed.

The 1970 study of urban officials conducted by the ACIR solicited a wide variety of information on local policy toward citizen participation. Specifically, the study asked questions concerning the number and type of participation activities in operation, the degree of citizen influence accorded each program, the various functions performed by each, and the attitudes and opinions of municipal officials toward the programs. In the following analysis, these data are used to construct the matrix of citizen intensity and program variety described in the previous chapter. That matrix, it will be recalled, is constructed of two dimensions: one indicating the variety of citizen participation programs adopted; the other measuring the intensity of citizen influence. The ACIR survey asked each official to indicate which, if any, of several major categories of citizen participation programs their city had adopted. These included neighborhood councils, little city halls, and multiservice centers. In the index construction, those cities which had adopted more differing kinds of these programs were ranked highest on the *program variety* dimension. Those cities adopting none of these three programs were assigned a score of 1 on this dimension, those adopting any one of the programs a 2, those adopting any two a 3, and those having all three programs were assigned a scale-score of 4.

The ACIR survey also asked each official to indicate the functions performed by citizens participating in each of these activities. The list of functions included the following:

1. Setting goals
2. Formulating general policies
3. Determining specific service levels
4. Reviewing program plans
5. Approving program plans
6. Determining multiservice center locations
7. Reviewing the budget
8. Monitoring service adequacy
9. Channeling citizen complaints
10. Hiring professional staff
11. Acting as advocates for citizens

Some of these functions, it will be noted, represent a greater degree of actual citizen influence than others. For example, the authority to approve program plans denotes a much more influential position vis-à-vis city hall than simply the ability to review program plans. In fact, argues Carl Stenberg—senior analyst of the ACIR—three of these functions are most indicative of the extent to which citizens are accorded real influence in the decentralization process. As he states, "the plan approval, budgetary review, and staffing functions are especially critical indicators of the degree to which real ... decentralization has taken place."[3]

Thus, in constructing the dimension measuring the extent of citizen influence (i.e., intensity), those programs in which citizens were involved in all three of these critical functions were ranked highest, those in which citizens were involved in two of these three were ranked second highest, and so forth. In addition, another factor—the method of citizen selection—was taken into account in the construction of this dimension.[4] Those programs in which citizen participants were elected from and by their neighborhood were ranked higher on this dimension than those in which citizens were appointed (either by the mayor, planning staff, or any other official body). Thus this dimension is, itself, a composite scale accounting for both the means of selection and degree of substantive influence. Such a procedure directly reflects the concerns of democratic theorists such as Hanna Pitkin and Paul Peterson who insist that in attempting to assess actual influence, one must consider both the concepts of *formal representation* ("the arrangements by which the representatives are selected") and *substantive representation* ("which takes into account the realm of action").[5] The intensity dimension of the matrix constructed for this study does account for both concerns.

Both dimensions (intensity and variety) were collapsed into four categories,[6] and the resulting sixteen-cell matrix of program intensity and variety appears in Figure 2-1.

Every United States city over 50,000 for which information is available (227) was then assigned an index score corresponding to its matrix location. As is commonly practiced in index construction of this sort, a city's score on this index is calculated simply by the following formula: Index Score $= A$ (where A equals the city's score on one dimension) $+ B$ (where B equals the city's score on the second dimension) $- 1$. The frequency distribution of the 227 cities on this index is presented in Chapter 3.

The reader will note that this procedure of index construction is similar to what Selltiz et al. label "differential scaling,"[7] and that such scales are always somewhat arbitrary since one assumes that scale scores of equal value are approximately equal in their representation of the "real world." However, such an assumption is not without conceptual problems. As the index constructed above clearly shows, a score of, say 3, actually stands for three different matrix locations and could be assigned either to a city receiving a 3 on either the variety or intensity dimension and a 1 on the other or to a city receiving a 2 on each dimension. This is, of course, a problem of validity, common to all scaling attempts. It is not argued here, nor can any scale guarantee, that cities receiving the same score may not in fact represent to some degree different program characteristics. It is suggested, and this is the major advantage of scale construction, that the resulting index does provide a more appropriate measure of the phenomenon being considered than can any single item. Selltiz and her associates even go on to argue that the problem described above is not as serious as it may first appear.

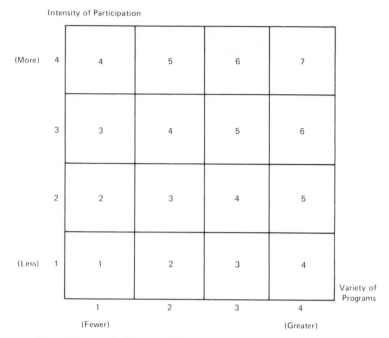

Figure 2-1. Matrix of Program Intensity and Variety.

The fact that different patterns of response may lead to identical scores [on this sort of scale] is not necessarily as serious a drawback as it may at first appear. Some of the differences in response patterns leading to a given score may be attributable to random variations in response. Thus some of the differences in response patterns leading to the same score may be thought of as error from the point of view of the attitude being measured, rather than as true differences in attitude that are being obscured by identical scores. Moreover, different ways of getting to the same place may be equivalent from the point of view of the measurement goal that is being served. For example, if one weights addition and subtraction equally in a concept of arithmetic ability, it makes sense to score two individuals as equivalent in arithmetic ability, even though one is relatively strong in addition and the other relatively strong in subtraction. Similarly, it may make sense to say that the net degree of animosity toward a given attitudinal object is the same in two individuals even though the animosity expresses itself differently.[8]

In addition to this scale (treated in Chapters 3 and 4 as the dependent variable) a number of socioeconomic and political factors, of course, are also examined in the attempt to determine which environments are most conducive to the varying participation activities. Many of these factors such as median income and education, city size, and so forth are derived from such standard sources as the United States Census of the Population and require no introduction. Others, however, are less frequently used (some are unique to this study) and the remainder of this section describes these variables.

One factor which is quite often thought to have significant consequences for urban politics is the degree of municipal reformism. The origins of the reform movement and its theoretical significance for programs of citizen involvement are discussed in Chapters 3 and 4. Here, a description of how the concept *reformism* is operationalized is presented. In general, it has been assumed that three measures of urban political structure are particularly significant indicators of the reform movement. These are the city manager form of government; nonpartisan politics; and at-large elections. In attempting to combine these three measures into a single variable of municipal reformism, essentially the same procedure as that adopted by Robert Lineberry and Edmond Fowler is used in the following analysis.[9] Lineberry and Fowler constructed a four-point index of municipal reformism ranging from those cities which had all three reform structures (coded 4) to those having none of these structures (coded 1). They admit that this is somewhat of a rough-and-ready index; yet conceptually the scale is of considerable utility, as will be demonstrated in Chapter 4. Data from which such an index is constructed is provided in the yearly publication of the International City Management Association.[10]

Moreover, it is often assumed that the legal or constitutional (charter) strength of the urban mayor is a variable likely to affect local politics. According to Robert Lineberry and Ira Sharkansky, "in a strong-mayor city, the mayor plays a more crucial role in both policy initiation and administration. He typically dominates the budget-formation process and key administrative appointments."[11] The mayor's power (at least legally speaking) generally is thought to be comprised of three measures: the method of mayoralty selection (by popular election or by council selection); his veto power; and his voting power. In some instances the mayor may veto all legislation, in others he can veto only budgetary measures, and in still others, he has no veto powers. Similarly, some mayors can vote on all issues, in some cases he can vote only in cases of ties, and in some cities he has no voting power. In Chapter 4 a scale of mayoralty strength is examined, comprised of these three legal sources of strength. Obviously, those mayors possessing all three powers (vote on all issues, veto any legislation, and elected by popular vote) are assigned the highest rating on the index of mayoralty strength.[12]

It has also been found that metropolitan fragmentation may significantly affect a city's policy process.[13] As ordinarily defined, *fragmentation* may mean either the total number of local governments within a single area or the per capita number of governments within the standard statistical metropolitan areas. Both indices of fragmentation are employed in the following analysis. Information from which these scales can be constructed is available in the United States Census of Governments and the Census of Population.

A final environmental factor unique to this study is a scale of the incidents and intensity of urban violence. As will be discussed in Chapter 4, it has been suggested by many that the degree of urban unrest may significantly affect a city's response to the citizen participation movement. Fortunately, an accurate account of all such incidents of urban disorder from 1965 through July 31, 1968 has been assembled and cataloged by the McClelland Subcommittee on Investigations of the United States Senate Committee on Governmental Operations.[14] As indicated in the report accompanying the publication of this information, the data were collected in the following manner:

Lists were compiled from various news media of all cities and towns which were reported to have experienced some sort of riot or civil disturbance. A letter and reporting form was directed from the chairman of the subcommittee to the mayor or city manager of each of these communities requesting basic statistics that would provide data to measure the scope of this national problem. Responses have been almost 100 percent. In those few instances where information could not be obtained from municipal officials, the staff compiled such statistics as were available from local news reports.[15]

Combined, the committee recorded thirteen incidents of urban disorder for every United States city during these years, including the number of law officers and civilians killed and/or injured, the type of criminality (sniping, looting, arson, etc.), the number of arrests, the amount of property damage involved, and so forth. In order to determine which of these items appeared to most accurately reflect an underlying dimension of urban violence, a Guttman scale-analysis routine was applied (by this author) to the data.[16] That procedure indicated that five of these items appeared to form a dimension of riot severity, as indicated in Table 2-1.

The Citizen Participation Survey of Twenty-Six Neighborhood Programs

The process model is concerned with the impact of public policy as well as its causes. This study is particularly concerned with the impact of citizen involvement activities on the neighborhood participant. In order to acquire the needed information, data were gathered, during a five-month period (October 1972 to February 1973), from 396 individuals participating in twenty-six neighborhood programs. The process of data collection, to be described below, was a combination of in-depth interviewing, questionnaire administration, and direct observation. The specific selection of programs for visitation and observation was a result of several influences. In the first place, the ACIR survey indicated which cities had initiated some form of citizen participation program. From this list, a group of midwestern programs was selected for analysis. These programs

Table 2-1
Guttman Scale-Analysis of Riot Disorders

Item	Scale Errors
Law officer or civilian killed?	14
National Guard employed?	17
Looting?	25
Injuries?	20
Vandalism?	8
CR = 0.90	

were not chosen on strictly a random basis. Such a selection procedure would have resulted in almost every program being ranked near the lower portion of the matrix (simply because the majority of programs throughout the country are narrow in scope and limited in participation intensity). Rather, the programs were selected so as to insure adequate representation of the programs as measured by the index of scope and intensity described below. Thus the selection process closely approximated the stratified-sampling method often used in survey research.[17]

As a matter of research convenience (i.e., taking into account such factors as travel time, research costs, accessibility, etc.), the programs sampled were limited to those operating in the Midwest, and the reader should understand the limitations inherent in generalizing from this sample to all programs in the United States. In fact, there is no attempt to suggest that the findings and conclusions based on this sample are necessarily applicable to all programs of neighborhood participation throughout the United States or even within the Midwest. At the same time, it is clear that limiting the survey to a single geographic section has its own methodological advantages. Urban scholars have often reported apparently important discoveries, only to find the magnitude of their relationships to be reduced significantly when section of the country was controlled.[18] Therefore, although the selection procedure employed here sacrifices whatever insights might result from an interregional comparison, at the same time it automatically controls for the possible confounding influences of region. Thus the process does allow greater confidence that whatever variance is observed in the dependent variables may be attributed solely to those forces of central concern to this study and is not influenced by variations in region. Still, the reader is cautioned from attempting to generalize beyond the regional confines of this study.

The twenty-six programs visited were operating in four states and six metropolitan areas (St. Louis, Missouri; Champaign, Illinois; Indianapolis, Indiana; Richmond, Indiana; Dayton, Ohio; and Lima, Ohio). Of the twenty-six programs, two were Project Area Committees funded by Urban Renewal funds, two were Community Action Programs funded by the Office of Economic Opportunity, ten were funded by Model Cities (or "planned variation") grants, and the remaining twelve received no direct federal funding. The majority of programs were operating in the inner-city section of the metropolitan areas, the average attendance was about seventeen neighborhood residents (although the range of attendance was as low as five to a high of forty), and most were racially segregated. Some of the members were elected by neighborhood elections, most attended on a self-selection basis, and a very few were appointed by the city's mayor.

In order to gain access to each program, a letter in early October 1972 was mailed to the chairman or president of each organization explaining the nature of the research and describing the needed information. This letter was followed by a phone call confirming the time, place, and date of the meeting and discussing at length with the chairman the activities performed by each program. Of all programs so contacted, two declined to participate in the study. These were replaced in the sample by organizations displaying characteristics as similar in demographic and structural makeup as possible. Prior to each visitation, in-depth, recorded, interviews were conducted with city officials dealing most closely with the programs.

Following these preliminary steps, a regularly-scheduled meeting of each program was attended. During this attendance (usually at the conclusion of each program), the participants were asked to complete a comprehensive survey of their attitudes, opinions, motives, and evaluations of the program. The survey, which took from fifteen to twenty minutes to complete, was administered by this researcher to the group as a whole. Each question from the survey was read to the group and each individual recorded his own response. This process of questionnaire administration, although time-consuming, not only tremendously increased the rate of questionnaire completion (which was almost 100%) over what would be expected from a mailed return, it also provided the researcher with an opportunity to become familiar, through personal inspection, with each program's activities. Such familiarity was necessary for the construction of the participation index.

In a manner similar to that described above (when considering the ICMA survey of all United States cities), these programs were ranked on a two-dimensioned array of participation intensity and program scope. To repeat, a composite score for each dimension was obtained by the following methods: interviews conducted with leaders of each program as well as informal discussions with other citizen participants; a personal, on-sight, visitation of each program; and recorded interviews with city officials. Based on these criteria, these programs were then ranked according to the following nine-celled matrix[19] (a frequency distribution is presented in Chapter 5) as shown in Figure 2-2.

Examples of programs receiving the highest score (5) on this matrix are the

Intensity of Citizen Participation

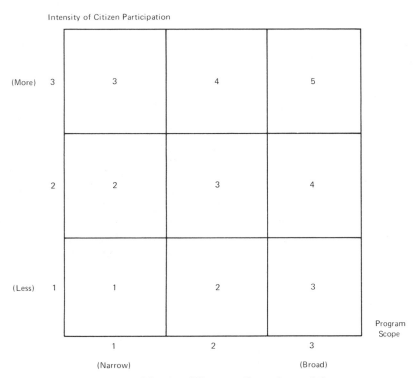

Figure 2-2. Matrix of Program Intensity and Scope.

priority boards initiated by the city of Dayton, Ohio. Each of these five boards consists of representatives annually elected by residents of their area of the city. The size of each board varies according to the population of the neighborhood and ranges from as few as twenty to as many as forty elected representatives. Each board is free to select its own officers and is provided staff assistance from city hall. Each board has as its responsibility the determination of how its annual grant, much of which is supplied through planned variations of Model Cities funds is to be spent. The size of each program's annual budget also varies by population of the neighborhood, but in 1972 averaged from 2 to 3 million dollars per program. The variety of programs in which the boards are involved include job training and placement, day-care centers, after-school recreation facilities, cable television negotiations, community police relations, senior citizens activities, zoning, education, and so forth. Although Dayton's city council (commission) retains the right of final approval over expenditures, for all practical purposes the city does not exercise its veto authority. Explaining the process of fund allocation and dispersion, a Dayton city official interviewed for this study stated:

They [the priority boards] are responsible for their grant, and in practical fact the priority boards have absolute power over the money they receive. The priority boards take a total plan to the commission for approval. . . . In fact, the commission does not object to what is in that plan. In no instance has the commission just vetoed a plan. In 99% of the cases, the commission just rubberstamps the plan.[20]

The ranking of Dayton's priority boards in terms of the matrix constructed above is corroborated by other studies of Dayton's programs. George Washnis, for example, found that "the boards can use the funds for whatever legal purpose they wish. The only thing turned down so far has been a request for a 'block party.' "[21] Likewise, in constructing her eight-rung ladder of participation, Sherry Arnstein assigned a rating of seven to Dayton's program, second only to what she labeled absolute neighborhood control.[22]

Examples of programs receiving the next highest rating (4) on this matrix are several umbrella programs established in the city of Indianapolis. These umbrella associations were formed in the various neighborhoods by neighborhood residents and each association represents several smaller organizations. The umbrella organizations are involved in as many differing sorts of activities as Dayton's priority boards, thus they receive the highest rating on the scope dimension. However, they rate somewhat lower than Dayton's programs in terms of association control of municipal and federal funds. Whereas Dayton's priority boards receive a block grant to be spent as they determine best, each project proposed by an Indianapolis umbrella organization seeking city controlled funds must receive separate approval. This process of approval is, itself, rather complicated with various municipal agencies and departments exercising varying degrees of influence throughout. As explained by a city official of Indianapolis whose department has as its primary function the monitoring of funds received and spent by these groups, the process operates (through 1972) as follows:

Our department solicits proposals for funding applications [from the various organizations]. Our staff then analyzes each request for internal consistency, feasibility, etc. and with representatives of community groups begin the process of weeding out. [In 1972], we had 2 1/2 times as many requests as we had money for. Also we felt open to fund a project for which we did not receive a request but for which we felt a need in the neighborhood. Through this process we cut the requests by half. There was an opportunity for appeal. We then made a final recommendation to the mayor who changed some of the recommendations, himself. Final approval then must come from the county council.[23]

Clearly, the amount of actual control exercised over the receipt and expenditure of funds received through municipal offices is less in Indianapolis than in Dayton. Whereas in Dayton each group receives a grant and, for all practical purposes, can spend that money unchallenged by city hall, Indianapolis has established a rigorous review process through which a number of municipal agencies can alter projects, veto requests, and even add programs for which no neighborhood organization requested funding. James Sundquist and David Davis have described two models of participation activities which very nearly capture the essential differences between the programs in Dayton and Indianapolis.[24] The first of these models (of which the programs in Dayton closely approximate) is described by Sundquist and Davis as one which to a considerable degree lacks central (i.e., city hall) direction and coordination but which is encouraged to "vigorously challenge the status quo, to innovate, and to raise a myriad of questions. . . ."[25] The Indianapolis program, on the other hand, closely resembles the second model described by Sundquist and Davis as one in which coordination of activities (rather than innovation) is stressed by city hall; planning is conducted by citizens *and* public authorities; and greater control is exercised throughout by the city administration. The implications of these models for those concerns of specific interest to this study are examined in Chapter 6.

Examples of programs rated lowest (1) on this matrix are Project Area Committees visited in Richmond, Indiana and Champaign, Illinois. These programs are ranked lowest on the scope dimension because of the narrow focus of their concern. As established by federal requirements for the receipt of Urban Renewal funds, each PAC is concerned only with housing rehabilitation (not even other concerns of Urban Renewal activities—such as redevelopment and conservation). These programs are rated lowest on the intensity dimension because their function is entirely advisory. Except for small monetary grants for secretarial functions, the programs receive no funds (the Richmond PAC claims that it did not even receive its total allocated supply grant for 1972). Government officials are not required to meet with the PACs except for "once during the first year that the PAC is established."[26] However, the most important fact, in terms of assigning an index value to these programs, is that their role is strictly advisory; city officials are under no compulsion to follow their wishes.

In this manner, each program visited was assigned an index value comprised of its ranking on the two dimensions of scope of coverage and intensity of participation. The resulting matrix is employed in this analysis as one factor likely associated with the various consequences of citizen participation activities.

As discussed above, in attempting to measure the consequences of these various program arrangements, participants in each neighborhood association were asked to complete a survey which was administered during the visitation of each program. In addition to the attitudinal and demographic data solicited from each participant, the questionnaire was designed also to measure each respondent's political trust and efficacy. The indices of efficacy and trust administered to each participant are comprised of the familiar questions included in the national election surveys conducted every other year by the Survey Research Center of the University of Michigan. In the chapters which follow, especially in

Chapter 6, these scales become important in attempting to assess the impact participation upon the neighborhood resident.

Summary

The data sets employed in this analysis represent the widest and most comprehensive surveys of citizen participation programs available. Through personal interviews and questionnaire administration, the attitudes and opinions of citizens participating in twenty-six programs, representing a wide variety of structural and social characteristics, are included. Some of these programs receive CAP or Model Cities funds, some receive Urban Renewal support, and some rely solely upon dues and contributions for their financing. In addition to this, the ACIR study permits the inclusion of information on citizen partici-pation programs gathered from city officials of 227 United States cities over 50,000 population. Combined with social and political data gathered from various governmental and official publications, these data sets permit the most thorough examination of those environments conducive to citizen participation activities as well as the most complete evaluation of the consequences of citizen involvement yet undertaken. Obviously, the approach to be followed sacrifices intensity of analysis (such as would be possible with a case-study approach) for extensive coverage. However, as Chapter 1 indicated, a sufficient number of case studies are available; the sorts of questions which urgently need answering can only be approached through an aggregate, comparative analysis. Therefore, an in-depth description of any single program is not attempted in this study; rather, the emphasis is upon exploring the consequences of differing structural and program arrangements among a wide range of citizen participation activities. The following chapter explores the social and economic correlates of the various citizen participation programs.

3

Citizen Participation and the Urban Environment

Students of both state and local politics have, in recent years, become increasingly interested in the exploration of the relationships between various socioeconomic conditions, political factors, and policy outputs. At the municipal level, this interest reflects, in part, a growing acceptance of the policy-process model as a method of policy analysis and, in part, a continued concern with possible cultural and ethnic influences upon municipal policy-making. This chapter, and the one which follows, examines the social, economic, and political factors associated with the various citizen participation programs in all United States cities over 50,000 for which data is available.

The policy-process model is now such an accepted method of policy analysis as to require little introduction. As is generally known, the model borrows heavily from the Eastonian systems approach to the study of politics[1] and suggests that, for analytical purposes, the basic elements of policy-making may be identified and that their separate and combined impacts upon policy outputs may be calculated. In common usage, the primary elements of the policy-process model include environmental influences (alternately called demands and supports); political factors (sometimes labeled "conversion processes"), the policy itself (policy output); and the impact of the policy upon its environment.[2]

Unquestionably, the application of the process model and its heavy reliance upon socioeconomic/political information has profoundly altered the nature of urban and state political research. In their review of recent state and local literature, Herbert Jacob and Michael Lipsky conclude that "the most marked innovation in the study of state and local politics has been the investigation of the relationship of policy outputs to social, economic, and political variables. . . . "[3] Likewise, in his review of the urban literature, Brett Hawkins concludes that "the urban field has experienced a shift in emphasis. Policy analysis now is being directed at hypotheses about environmental and system determinates. . . . "[4] Indeed, investigations using this approach have produced a number of important (Jacob and Lipsky claim "startling") results. It has been shown, for example, by both students of state and local politics that many political and structrual variables (such as form of local government,[5] legislative apportionment,[6] party competition,[7] etc.) previously considered important appear to have less of an effect on various policy outcomes than socioeconomic variables.

In spite of its contributions to state and local policy analysis, the policy-process model has several limitations as it has been applied in most previous research.[8] Two of the most important of these concern the conceptual problem of categorizing those policy outputs to be examined and the methodological problem of multicollinearity existing among the independent (i.e., input) variables. The analysis presented here attempts to examine this single policy, citizen participation programs, through the application of the policy-process model and, by avoiding these two limitations, at the same time seeks a better understanding of the policy process itself.

Most previous policy research, because of the nature of available information, has relied heavily upon measures of fiscal spending as output variables. Measures commonly used in this type of research include such variables as proportion of municipal budget allocated to planning concerns,[9] per capita expenditures on education, welfare, and health,[10] and other estimates of fiscal output. Since levels of spending obviously are related to measures of affluence (ability to pay), it is not surprising that so many studies have found strong socioeconomic and weak political correlations with measures of fiscal policy. As William Shaffer and Ronald Weber have noted in a recent paper, "the previous research upon . . . policy making, which has found that states tend to respond with the highest level of fiscal policy output when they have a wealthy resource base, seems to have tested inappropriately the process assumption. *For when policy outputs are measured using level of spending, it seems patently obvious that a unit of government cannot spend at high levels if it does not possess the resources to spend at that level.*"[11] Clearly, it is possible that many of the findings of those employing the policy-process framework may be tempered when more studies of nonfiscal outputs are available. In their study of several nonfiscal policy outputs among the fifty states, in fact, Weber and Shaffer found that, although political variables were not significant in every case, important relationships were found to exist between political variables and such policies as teacher unionization and gun control legislation.[12] The present study, then, adds an important dimension to urban policy research: the examination of social, economic, and political influences upon the nonfiscal policy of citizen participation activities. It should be of interest to discover if those relationships reported in previous research using fiscal measures remain intact.[13]

In addition, most previous policy research has failed to consider the problem of multicollinearity among the independent variables employed in their studies.[14] The basic problem is that highly correlated variables (such as per capita income, education, industrialization, etc.) may actually be reflecting one underlying dimension (such as affluence), and the inclusion of each in the analysis may result in highly unstable partial correlations as well as depressing the significance of other independent variables.[15] In attempting to reduce this risk, later sections of this study rely upon factor analysis as a technique to discern from among several possible independent variables the underlying (and independent) dimensions of importance.

Also, for a second and more traditional reason, urban scholars are interested in the social, political, and economic factors associated with policy outputs. This is the continuing interest which students of local politics have expressed in the cultural and ethnic influences upon urban policy.[16] For the most part this interest is attributed to the Edward Banfield and James Wilson ethos theory.[17] According to that theory, much of urban politics can be understood in terms of two prevalent attitudinal syndroms—one they label as "private-regarding," the other "public-regarding." Private-regarding attitudes, they say, are oriented toward personal politics, involving a political style "not unlike that provided by the political machine."[18] The public-regarding attitude supposedly represents a view associated with such values as honesty, professionalism, and efficiency. In addition, according to Banfield and Wilson, each of these orientations toward politics is associated with objective class and ethnic considerations. The middle and upper classes, they believe, are most likely to express public-regarding attitudes, the lower and immigrant classes are most likely to express private-regarding values. They state:

There is a tendency for [urban cleavages] to coalesce into two opposite patterns. These patterns reflect two conceptions of the public interest that are widely held. The first, which derives from the middle class ethos, favors what the municipal reform movement has always defined as "good government"—namely efficiency, impartiality, honesty, planning, strong executives, no favoritism, model legal codes, and strict enforcement of laws against gambling and vice. The other conception of the public interest (one never explicitly formulated as such, but one all the same) derives from the "immigrant ethos." *This is the conception of those people who identify with the ward or neighborhood rather than the city* . . . who look to politicians for "help" and "favors," . . . and who are far less interested in the efficiency, impartiality, and honesty of local government than in its readiness to confer material benefits of one sort or another upon them.[19]

It should be mentioned that Banfield and Wilson are not the only, or even the first, scholars to espouse this interpretation of urban politics. Earlier, Richard Hofstadter presented a similar cultural interpretation of urban politics.

Out of the clash between the needs of the immigrants and the sentiments of the natives there emerged two thoroughly different systems of political ethics. One, founded upon the indigenous Yankee-Protestant political traditions, and upon middle-class life, assumed and demanded the constant, disinterested activity of the citizen in public affairs. . . . The other system, founded upon the European backgrounds of the immigrants . . . interpreted political and civic relations chiefly in terms of personal obligations, and placed strong personal loyalties above allegiance to abstract codes of law or morals. It was chiefly upon this system of values that the political life of the immigrant, the boss, and the urban machine was based.[20]

Robert Binstock described municipal reform in Worcester, Massachusetts in similar terms. According to Binstock, "Yankees are the cultural, business, and social leaders—in short, 'the first families of Worcester.' "[21]

Other examples of cultural interpretations of urban politics could be mentioned.[22] The point to be stressed here is that each of these suggest that the intercity variations in political policies and structures can, to some degree, be explained in terms of cultural and ethnic characteristics. Banfield and Wilson formulate the most explicit set of structures and policies likely to be associated with each attitude. Concerning the middle-class orientation of public-regardingness, they state:

The logic of the middle-class ideal requires that authority be exercised by those who are 'best qualified' that is, technical experts. . . . The logic implies also certain institutional arrangements (non-partisanship, at-large election, the council manager form, master planning, and metropolitan area organization).[23]

Others have tested these relationships, but the results are somewhat contradictory. Some have found that, as the cultural thesis suggests, political structures such as the city manager form of government, nonpartisan politics, and at-large elections are positively related to: white-collar occupations,[24] higher median-value housing,[25] lower percentage foreign born,[26] lower percentage over sixty-five,[27] higher percentage completing high school,[28] higher median family income,[29] higher percentage of families in one-family housing units.[30]

Others, however, dispute these findings. Most notable is the comprehensive study of Wolfinger and Field who argue that, while on the surface these relationships seem to exist, they largely disappear when area of the country is controlled for. These scholars conclude that the ethos theory, if it is to be of any value, is badly in need of revision.[31]

It is suggested here that the decision to adopt or not to adopt a citizen participation program (and if so, what form of program) offers an ideal test of the cultural thesis. Clearly, citizen participation in public affairs is contrary to the principles of economy, efficiency, and professionalism attributed to middle- and upper-class (public-oriented) values. This argument, although yet to be empirically tested, has been made by several students of municipal politics and administration. Stenberg, for example, notes that "citizen involvement is commonly thought to be antithetical to much of public administration and practice. In this sense, there is a built-in conflict between citizen participation and the *middle class values* of bureaucrats, the objectives of the merit system, and the traditional principles of hierarchy and professionalism found in American administrative thought."[32] Likewise, Joseph Zimmerman finds that "the new reform [citizen participation] differs sharply with the views of the early twentieth-century [middle-class] reformers who were interested in cleaning up corruption and creating a city government capable of providing services in the most economical and efficient manner."[33] As a final example, Alan Altshuler finds that "most intellectuals and social science critiques of community control believe that it would be inimical to governmental honesty, equity, and professionalism."[34] It is reasonable, then, to suppose that those environments which Banfield and Wilson suggest will be associated with those programs reflecting middle- and upper-class values will be related to citizen participation programs *in an opposite manner*. The determination of which environments, if any, are most associated with citizen participation activities should add further empirical evidence to support or refute the cultural hypothesis.

Thus it is argued above that an analysis of the social, economic, and political factors associated with citizen participation programs will serve more than simply determining which environments are most conducive to citizen participation activities (although that in itself should be of interest). In the first place, by using techniques similar to the policy-process model, the analysis should present a better understanding of the process itself. In particular, as was noted above, most prior research of the urban policy process relying on *fiscal* measures as indicators of policy output have reported socioeconomic influences to be more important than political factors. It should be of interest to determine if this relationship remains valid when a *nonfiscal* measure of output is employed. Secondly, it is obvious that, as a policy to be pursued, cities differ in their acceptance of citizen participation programs. Some have initiated no program, some have sponsored very limited citizen participation activities, and some have developed programs approaching neighborhood control of a wide variety of activities. There is, in addition, a body of theory linking various socioeconomic environments to variations in municipal policy, and the examination of which environments are most conducive to citizen participation programs should provide an ideal test of this theory. The analysis presented in this chapter explores three general questions. First, how do cities in general differ (in terms of city size, region, and metropolitan type) in their response to the citizen participation movement? Second, what ethnic, racial, and social characteristics are associated with the various citizen participation programs? Third, to what extent do whatever social and ethnic relationships which may be discovered appear to be attributable to cultural differences (and thus supportive of the ethos theory) rather than other factors?

The Dependent Variable

As mentioned in the previous chapter, in the construction of the dependent variable, all United States cities over 50,000 for which information is available were arrayed along a two-dimensioned matrix.[35] One dimension of that matrix represents the variety of programs adopted by each city, the other represents the intensity (degree) of actual citizen involvement (see Chapter 2 for a more precise explanation of this matrix). The resulting matrix allows for seven possible scale scores along which the cities are ranked. Table 3-1 presents the frequency distribution of these cities along this scale.

Table 3-1
The Citizen Participation Scale

Citizen Participation Index	Number of Cities	Percentage of Total
1	107	47.1%
(No citizen participation program)		
2	25	11.0
3	45	19.8
4	29	12.8
5	16	7.0
6	5	2.2
7	0	0.0
(Greatest variety and intensity)		
	N = 227	100.0

As Table 3-1 indicates, almost half (47.1 percent) of the cities over 50,000 have initiated no citizen participation program at all. Moreover, none of the cities reported an effort which would have rated 7 on the scale of variety and intensity (such a rating would allow a neighborhood almost total control over a wide variety of activities). This scale of variety and intensity is used as the dependent variable in this, and the following, chapter.

Citizen Participation and Region,
City Size, and Type

A general overview of the variations in citizen participation activities by size, region, and metropolitan type is of interest for several reasons. In the first place, such an analysis should tend to confirm (or reject) interpretations of the practical motivations of those supporting citizen participation programs outlined in Chapter 1. It was argued in that chapter that such programs offer solutions both to those citizens traditionally isolated from the municipal decision-making process and to those officials concerned with urban disorders. Thus it would be assumed that citizen participation activities would be found mostly in larger central cities. Indeed, in his study of twenty CAAs, David Austin found that the most important factor associated with intensity of participation was city size.[36] Also, Carl Stenberg found in his study that "central cities are far more likely to have decentralized services . . . than suburban and independent jurisdictions."[37] In addition, such an analysis is of interest because of its direct significance for the ethos theory described above. Noting the seeming correspondence between reformed political structures (such as the manager form of government) and city size, Banfield and Wilson state that larger cities will be less likely to adopt measures reflecting public-oriented values because "the larger the city, generally speaking, the more is at stake politically, and consequently the greater the effort that . . . politicians will put forth to avoid being displaced." Banfield and Wilson go on to argue that, although a negative correlation between size and reform measures should be evident, "it is not the size of the city per se which has made the difference; rather it is the empirical correlation between large size and the relative number and political power of the lower class."[38] In any case, the Banfield and Wilson thesis would suggest that the larger, inner cities should score highest on the citizen participation index.

Competing with the Banfield and Wilson thesis as a predictor of the relationship between metropolitan type (inner city or suburban) and citizen participation activities is the argument developed by Robert Wood who suggests that it is in suburbia where one might expect the greatest agitation for programs of citizen involvement. Wood compares the political ideology of suburbanites and city dwellers and finds that "the justification of suburban legal independence rests on the classic belief in grassroots democracy, our long-standing conviction that small political units represent the purest expression of popular rule, that the government closest to home is best."[39] Such a philosophy, he says, leads to a "strong sense of community consciousness and civic responsibility that impels active participation in local affairs."[40] And, he claims that it is in the suburb where one finds that "the image of resurrected grassroots democracy commits the citizen, theoretically at least, to a do-it-yourself brand of politics. . . ."[41] Wood's thesis is, of course, also examined in this analysis.

Also, region is of interest because others have argued that many of the relationships tending to support the ethos theory are significantly reduced when area of the country is controlled.[42] The hypotheses to be tested in Table 3-2, then, are as follows:

Hyp. 1: As city size increases, the ranking on the citizen participation index will increase.

Hyp. 2: Citizen participation activities will more likely be found in inner city (rather than suburban) areas.

Hyp. 3: Significant regional variations in the citizen participation index may be observed (if region, not culture, is the critical factor).

Table 3-2 reveals some very interesting relationships. In the first place, region is of very little importance in discriminating between the various levels of participation. Although others (especially Wolfinger and Field) have noted a strong correlation between region and various reformed structures, there is almost no relationship between region and the initiation of citizen participation programs. Although fewer cities in the Far West have adopted citizen participation activities than those in other areas, the difference fails to meet the 0.05

Table 3-2
Citizen Participation and Region, City Size, and Metropolitan Type

Participation Matrix	Region				Size				Metropolitan Type	
	Northeast	South	Midwest	Farwest	50,000-100,000	100,000-250,000	250,000-500,000	Over 500,000	Inner City[a]	Suburban
1	43.5%	38.6%	42.6%	61.9%	59.1%	30.4%	19.0%	9.1%	36.1%	67.1%
2	10.9	12.3	11.5	9.5	12.8	8.7	4.8	9.1	11.1	11.8
3	21.7	17.5	21.3	19.0	17.4	34.8	14.3	0.0	22.9	13.2
4	10.9	15.8	16.4	7.9	8.1	13.0	23.8	54.5	15.3	7.9
5	10.9	12.3	4.9	1.6	2.0	8.7	28.6	27.3	11.1	0.0
6	2.2	3.5	3.3	0.0	0.7	4.3	9.5	0.0	3.5	0.0
	100.0	100.0	100.0	100.0	100.0	100.0	100.0	100.0	100.0	100.0
	(N = 46)	(N = 57)	(N = 61)	(N = 63)	(N = 149)	(N = 46)	(N = 21)	(N = 11)	(N = 144)	(N = 76)

Significance Level = (N.S.)

Significance Level = (0.001)
Tau C = 0.31

Significance Level = (0.001)

[a]The term *inner city* reflects the terminology adopted by the International City Management Association and is equivalent in meaning to the term *central city*.

level of significance. Especially interesting (although, again, the differences are not statistically significant) is the fact that a larger proportion of cities in the South have adopted some form of citizen participation program than in any other region. Except for the Far West, the cities of the South have adopted proportionally fewer of those structures considered to reflect the private regarding ethos (such as ward elections, partisan politics, etc.) than any other region.[43] Nevertheless, the most important fact concerning the relationship between region and the participation matrix is that the adoption of such programs are fairly evenly distributed throughout the various sections of the country.

Also compatible with the Banfield and Wilson ethos theory, Table 3-2 indicates that city size is an important predictor of the various types of participation programs. As that table shows, 59 percent of those cities between 50,000 and 100,000 have adopted no participation activity whereas only 9 percent of those cities over 500,000 have adopted no program of citizen involvement. Although, as Stenberg suggests, "decentralization is not just a big-city phenomenon,"[44] it is clear that the majority of all citizen participation activities, and especially those displaying more intense levels of citizen involvement, exist in the larger cities.

Just as pronounced is the difference between the attitudes of suburban and inner-city areas toward citizen participation. Contrary to what one might have expected applying Wood's thesis, Table 3-2 demonstrates that 67 percent of those cities classified as suburban have adopted no participation program, whereas 64 percent of those classified as central city have adopted some form of citizen involvement (Tau $C = -0.35$). This, of course, does not necessarily deflate Wood's central thesis—that suburbanites feel more of a sense of obligation to participate in civic affairs than those living in central cities. These results could simply be interpreted as showing that suburbanites are generally satisfied with their present participation opportunities.

The results presented so far tend to be consistent with what would be expected if the ethos theory were accurate. That is, larger and central cities, which tend to have larger proportions of lower-class inhabitants, are much more likely than smaller and suburban cities to adopt a program of citizen participation. In addition, the degree of intensity of actual citizen involvement is likely to be much greater in these same cities. It was also noted that region, a variable which others have found to significantly detract from findings supportive of the ethos theory, was of almost no importance. Banfield and Wilson suggest that these differences can be explained by the ethnic and especially class differences existing between large and small, inner and suburban, cities. The next sections examine more closely these relationships.

Ethnicity and Citizen Participation

In terms of the ethos theory, the independent effect of ethnicity on citizen participation is, obviously, a very important consideration. Although Banfield and Wilson never clarify the proportionate weight which should be attributed to class and ethnicity, it is clear that ethnicity is viewed by them as an important controlling variable. Discussing the impact of class and ethnicity on values, Banfield and Wilson remark, "We do not think that income per se has this effect [making people public- or private-regarding]; rather it is the ethnic attributes . . . empirically associated with it."[45]

Indeed, a number of studies have shown that ethnic composition is closely related to those reform political structures (such as city manager, at-large elections, and nonpartisan politics) which the cultural theory would predict would be associated with the public-regarding ethos. Robert Alford and Harry Scoble found foreign percentage to be associated with the mayor (unreformed) form of government.[46] They concluded that ethnic groups are important sources of social heterogeneity related to form of government."[47] Robert Lineberry and Edmond Fowler report that cities having all three of the unreformed political institutions (mayor form of government, ward elections, partisan politics) are more likely to be found in cities having larger proportions of ethnic populations.[48] Thus the two hypotheses concerning the effect of ethnicity on citizen participation activites tested in Table 3-3 are as follows:

Hyp. 4: The greater the proportion of foreign born, the higher the rank on the citizen participation index.

Hyp. 5: The greater the percentage of total foreign stock, the higher the rank on the citizen participation index.

As Table 3-3 indicates, there is only a very weak relationship between

Table 3-3
Citizen Participation and Ethnicity

Participation Matrix	Percentage Foreign Born:				Percentage Ethnic Stock:			
	Less than 1.0%	1.0-5.0 %	5.0-10.0 %	Over 10.0%	Less than 10.0%	10.0-20.0 %	20.0-30.0 %	Over 30.0%
1	60.0%	40.3%	58.8%	29.3%	45.6%	45.8%	56.3%	41.2%
2	15.0	9.7	8.8	14.6	11.4	14.6	6.3	11.8
3	15.0	20.8	19.1	19.5	17.7	27.1	18.7	17.6
4	7.5	16.7	5.9	22.0	16.5	8.3	6.3	17.6
5	0.0	11.1	2.9	14.6	6.3	4.2	6.3	11.8
6	2.5	1.4	4.4	0.0	2.5	0.0	6.3	0.0
	100.0	100.0	100.0	100.0	100.0	100.0	100.0	100.0
	(N = 40)	(N = 72)	(N = 68)	(N = 41)	(N = 79)	(N = 48)	(N = 48)	(N = 51)

Significance Level = (0.05)   Significance Level = (N.S.)
Tau C = 0.09

ethnicity and the citizen participation measure. It was found that the relation-ship between the percentage of foreign born and the citizen participation index was significant at the 0.05 level, however Tau C (0.09) indicates that the strength of that relationship is very slight. It is also shown in Table 3-3 that the hypothesized relationship between total foreign stock and the citizen partici-pation matrix failed to meet the test of significance at the 0.05 level.

Social class and Citizen Participation

Social class is also an important variable in the ethos theory. As discussed above, the thesis suggests that the private-regarding attitude, which gives rise to unreformed political institutions, is associated with lower-class as well as ethnic traits. Banfield, especially, in his more recent writings seems to place greater emphasis on the "imperatives of class." In one work Banfield states, "Within the limits set by the logic of growth, the mix of class cultures more than anything else determines the city's [political] character. . . . "[49] Consistent with those structures supposedly associated with private-regarding attitudes, then, one would hypothesize that citizen participation programs would be associated with cities displaying greater proportions of lower-class inhabitants. Class, of course, is a complex variable, comprised both of subjective and objective elements. However, three measures of class: percentage of white collar, median family income, and median school years, are most often used in the urban literature.[50] These same measures are used to examine the relationship between social class and the matrix of participation.[51] The following hypotheses are tested in Table 3-4:

Hyp. 6: The higher the median level of income, the lower the ranking on the citizen participation index.
Hyp. 7: The higher the proportion of white collar, the lower the ranking on the citizen participation matrix.
Hyp. 8: The higher the median education, the lower the ranking on the participation scale.

Table 3-4 indicates that those class variables which the ethos theory would suggest should be related to citizen participation activities only very weakly discriminate between those programs. Of the three class variables considered, median school years completed and proportion of residents in white-collar positions failed to meet the tests of statistical significance. Only the relationship between median income and the citizen participation matrix was statistically significant (in the proposed direction), however Tau C indicates the strength of that relationship to be very slight (-0.13).

The above analysis has shown that, although city size is related to partici-

Table 3-4
Citizen Participation and Social Class

Participation Matrix	Percentage in White-Collar Occupations				Median Family Income				Median School Years Completed			
	Less than 40%	40-45%	45-50%	Over 50%	Less than $5000	5000-6000	6000-7000	Over 7000	Less than 10.0	10.0-11.0	11.0-11.5	More than 11.5
1	48.0%	39.2%	51.8%	48.5%	55.3%	29.4%	45.1%	74.4%	40.0%	35.0%	56.7%	53.1%
2	10.0	7.8	8.9	16.2	7.9	16.2	11.0	5.1	12.5	15.0	6.7	10.2
3	18.0	17.6	21.4	22.1	15.8	23.5	20.7	15.4	17.5	15.0	16.7	22.4
4	12.0	21.6	10.7	7.4	18.4	13.2	14.6	2.6	20.0	17.5	6.7	10.2
5	10.0	7.8	7.1	4.4	2.6	11.8	7.3	2.6	7.5	10.0	13.3	3.1
6	2.0	5.9	0.0	1.5	0.0	5.9	1.2	0.0	2.5	7.5	0.0	1.0
	100.0	100.0	100.0	100.0	100.0	100.0	100.0	100.0	100.0	100.0	100.0	100.0
	(N = 50)	(N = 51)	(N = 56)	(N = 68)	(N = 38)	(N = 68)	(N = 82)	(N = 39)	(N = 40)	(N = 40)	(N = 30)	(N = 98)

Significance Level = (N.S.) (White-Collar Occupations)

Significance Level = (0.01)
Tau C = −0.13 (Median Family Income)

Significance Level = (N.S.) (Median School Years Completed)

pation activities in the direction suggested by the cultural theory of urban politics, the central environmental elements of that theory—ethnicity and class—are only very weakly related to the participation index. However, it may be too soon to conclude that the cultural thesis is of no value in explaining citizen participation programs. In a few instances, the relationships were found to be in the direction suggested by the ethos theory. In addition, some have suggested that structural, as well as environmental, factors should be examined in any test of the ethos theory. Lineberry and Fowler, for example, found that structural variables (reformism), but not environmental factors, were related to policy output. Thus they conclude that "an attitude [ethnic and cultural] structure may be less helpful in explaining the city's public policy than the characteristics of the institutions themselves. These conclusions are generally consistent with the ethos theory developed by Banfield and Wilson."[52] The effect of these structural variables on citizen participation activities are examined in Chapter 4 and a final evaluation of the ethos theory as a predictor of participation activities is reserved until then. The remainder of this chapter explores the relationship between participation and race and examines in greater detail the few environmental relationships which appear to be in the direction suggested by the ethos theory.

Race and Citizen Participation

A number of scholars have commented on the possible relationships between race and citizen participation activities. Douglas Yates speculates that "in cities with a small black percentage of the population, the critical mass of political power will be missing that is needed to force government in the direction of local participation."[53] Indeed, one earlier study has reported a relationship between proportions of the population black and citizen participation activities. In his study of twenty CAAs, Austin found that, other than size, "the most important factor [in explaining degrees of citizen participation] was the proportion of black residents in the central city."[54] The hypothesis tested in Figure 3-1, then, is as follows:

Hyp. 9: The greater the proportion of black residents, the higher the ranking on the citizen participation scale.

As indicated in Figure 3-1, a moderate relationship between proportion black and the citizen participation index is evident; the larger the proportion of black residents, the higher the score on the participation scale. Also, as Austin discovered in his analysis of twenty CAAs, the Tau C measure of strength of relationship indicates that the percentage black is second in importance only to city size. Important also, it seems, is the fact that citizen participation is not *just*

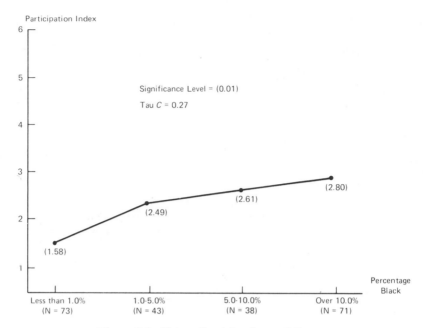

Figure 3-1. Citizen Participation and Race.

associated with larger black populations. Implicit in much of the literature is the assumption that citizen participation is solely or largely a quest confined to the black community and that whites, in general, are hostile (or at least indifferent) to such a reform. Altshuler, for example, says that decentralization and citizen involvement is "the most controversial item on the *black* agenda"[55] and devotes his entire book to convincing whites of the desirability of such programs. At the conclusion of his study, Altshuler states, "I need hardly add that the force of white resistance has been ever in my mind, shaping my view of which options were even worth discussing."[56] Although, as Figure 3-1 makes clear, a positive relationship between proportion black and the participation index does exist, still 32 percent of those cities reporting less than 1 percent black have initiated some participation program (however these on the average rank lower on the participation scale). In general, it appears that although race is one of the more important environmental variables examined in this chapter, other factors are involved in the citizen participation movement.

Class and Ethnicity Controlling for Size, Race, and City Type

The above analysis has indicated that those environmental factors which the ethos thesis would predict should be associated with citizen participation activities appear less important than other variables considered—particularly city size, racial composition, and metropolitan type. Nevertheless, in a few instances, the relationships as predicted by the ethos theory seemed to exist. This is especially true concerning the proportion of urban residents foreign born and the median family income of the various cities. Given the strength of the relationships between city size, percentage black, and the matrix of participation, it is appropriate to reexamine these relationships to determine what proportion of the variance in the participation index may be explained by these cultural variables when race, size, and city type are controlled. Table 3-5 presents this analysis.

As Table 3-5 indicates, when the relationships between the various cultural variables and citizen participation activities are examined *within* the various racial and size categories, these controls eliminate most of the remaining cultural relationships uncovered above. Of the sixty possible ethnic and cultural relationships presented in Table 3-5, only five (those between the citizen participation index and median income within cities between 50,000 and 100,000 population, total foreign stock within cities between 100,000 and 250,000, percentage of foreign born and median education in the suburbs, and percentage of foreign born within cities of over 10 percent black) remain significant at the 0.05 level. Clearly, the cultural and ethnic explanation of the citizen participation movement, as measured in this chapter, is of very limited utility.

Interesting also is the apparent reduction of the strong relationship between metropolitan type, proportion of black, and city size and the citizen participation index when controlling for each other. As Table 3-5 indicates, the relationship between percentage black and the participation scale remains significant only within those cities of between 50,000 and 100,000 and the relationship between size and the involvement index remains significant only when percentage black is greater than 5 percent. These relationships, however, are probably due to a considerable amount of covariation among these three variables. As mentioned at the beginning of this chapter, city size, metropolitan type, and proportion black may very well represent a single environmental dimension, and controlling for one while examining the others is of very little theoretical use. This proposition is tested more fully in the following chapter. The salient conclusion to be drawn from the data presented above is that city size and metropolitan type (and, to some extent, percentage black) are much better predictors of a city's ranking on the matrix of participation than any other environmental factors. In this regard, the results of this chapter substantiate those of other scholars (such as Wolfinger and Field) who have found that cultural explanations of urban policy and political structures are of little predictive value. Table 3-6 summarizes the relationships between the citizen participation index and the various environmental factors presented above.

As Table 3-6 indicates, the multiple correlation coefficient between these environmental factors and citizen participation activities is 0.44. The partial correlation coefficients once again clearly demonstrate that all those variables assumed to represent elements of the cultural or ethos theory (percentage

Table 3-5
Citizen Participation and Ethnicity, and Class Controlling for City Size, Race, and Metro Type

	Control Variables									
	City Size				Percentage Black				Metropolitan Type	
Independent Variables	50,000-100,000	100,000-250,000	250,000-500,000	Over 500,000	Less than 1.0%	1.0-5.0%	5.0-10.0%	Over 10.0%	Inner City	Suburban
% employed in white collar	N.S.	N.S.	N.S.	N.S.	N.S.	N.S.	N.S.	N.S.	N.S.	N.S.
Median income	-0.14[a]	N.S.	N.S.	N.S.	N.S.	N.S.	N.S.	N.S.	N.S.	N.S.
Median school	N.S.	N.S.	N.S.	N.S.	N.S.	N.S.	N.S.	N.S.	N.S.	-0.20[a]
% Foreign born	N.S.	N.S.	N.S.	N.S.	N.S.	N.S.	N.S.	0.17[a]	N.S.	0.20[a]
Total foreign stock	N.S.	0.13[a]	N.S.	N.S.	N.S.	N.S.	N.S.	N.S.	N.S.	N.S.
% Black	0.20[a]	N.S.	N.S.	N.S.	–	–	–	–	N.S.	0.16[a]
Metro type	N.S.	N.S.	–	–	N.S.	N.S.	N.S.	N.S.	–	–
City size	–	–	–	–	N.S.	N.S.	0.45[a]	0.28[b]	0.33[b]	N.S.

[a]Significance Level = 0.05
[b]Significance Level = 0.01

Table 3-6
Coefficients of Simple and Partial Correlation between Citizen Participation Index and Environmental Influences

Independent Variables	Simple r	Partial r
Percentage employed in white collar	−0.01	−0.05
Median family income	−0.04	0.05
Median school	0.02	−0.01
Percentage foreign born	0.07	0.07
Total foreign stock	0.04	−0.03
Percentage black	0.23	0.09
Metropolitan type (inner city or suburban)	−0.34	−0.26
City size (population)	0.31	0.18
	$R = 0.442$	
	$R^2 = 0.195$	

employed in white-collar occupations, median income and education, percentage foreign born, and total foreign stock) are of little predictive value when considering participation policy. The total amount of variance in the participation measure explained by all these socioeconomic and environmental factors is shown to be almost 20 percent (obviously the bulk of this can be accounted for by the two variables of metropolitan type and city size).

Summary: Citizen Participation and the Urban Environment

It was demonstrated at the outset that the citizen participation policies of cities vary widely. Almost half of the 227 cities examined in this study have initiated no form of citizen participation activity, and the rest have adopted programs dispersed along the participation matrix of scope and variety. It was noted also that this variance presents interesting questions for the urban scholar both in terms of the policy-process model and the relationships of various environments to citizen involvement. Chapter 4 more closely examines citizen participation in terms of the policy-process model and, in particular, examines the comparative importance of socioeconomic and political variables. However, it was noted above that those environmental factors generally used as measures of affluence (such as median income, education, proportion white collar, etc.) were of very little predictive value when considering the nonfiscal policy of citizen involvement. Thus it would be concluded that, at least when the nonfiscal measure of citizen participation policy is examined, the strong relationship which others have observed between measures of affluence and policy output is negligible. It is suggested that other studies of nonfiscal output measures may produce similar results.

It was also suggested that, at the urban level, a body of theory exists linking various environmental variables to policy concerns. This theory (alternately called the ethos or cultural thesis) suggests that various ethnic and class groups will display differing value orientations which will influence their policy choices. In particular, some have argued that those cities with large concentrations of lower-class and ethnic populations will be more prone to adopt citizen participation programs than other cities. It was demonstrated above that such a thesis of cultural determinism is of almost no predictive value concerning citizen participation activities. Although a few of these sorts of variables seemed to display significant relationships with programs of citizen involvement, those relationships faded to insignificance in almost every instance when city size, race, and metropolitan type were controlled.

This chapter has also shown that the most important environmental factors associated with citizen involvement are city size, race, and metropolitan type (suburban or inner city). Although the significance of the relationships between race, size, and citizen participation were reduced when controlling for metropolitan type, it was argued that these variables may represent a single dimension of metropolitanism and that controlling for one while examining the other is deceiving. The following chapter explores further this proposition.

Although these findings tend to significantly deflate the cultural explanation of citizen participation activities, they do little to explain why such factors as size, and to some extent race and metropolitan type, display such strong positive relationships with citizen involvement. On the one hand, these relationships are almost intuitively obvious since, as argued in Chapter 1, citizen participation is likely to appeal mainly to groups seeking a more favorable allocation of municipal services (such as inner-city blacks) and to political leaders seeking a reduction of urban tensions. At the same time, a number of political variables associated with city size may also display significant relationships. It has sometimes been suggested, for example, that mayors (who are found predominately in larger cities) will encourage the development of citizen participation programs in hopes of bolstering their organized political power. Others have suggested that the fragmentation of governments existing in larger cities is a force encouraging the initiation of citizen participation programs. Chapter 4 explores the relationship of these and other political variables to citizen involvement activities.

4

Citizen Participation and Urban Politics

It was found in the previous chapter that the combined impact of those socioeconomic variables generally thought to be significant predictors of urban policy accounted for almost 20 percent of the total variance in the participation index. Obviously, a focus on socioeconomic variables alone leaves a substantial portion of the participation variance unexplained. The primary questions to be pursued in this chapter are: How much more of this variance can be accounted for when political factors are included in the analysis? And, What is the *relative* predictive strength of political and socioeconomic influences?

At first, it might seem unusual that a study of a municipal public policy should have to test for a relationship between urban political variations and the policy being examined. Political scientists have for years, as Brett Hawkins states, "emphasized behavior within the political system and the characteristics of the system."[1] Yet, as indicated previously, contemporary applications of the policy-process model to the study of urban politics has seriously questioned the independent impact which system variables may have. Most of these have found, instead, that environmental factors appear to be far more important determinants of policy outcomes. However, it was also noted above that the process model as generally applied has been seriously criticized and that one of the most basic criticisms is the tendency by most to rely solely on fiscal measures of policy output. Not only should the examination of citizen participation (a nonfiscal policy) using the process model indicate which political environments are most conducive to citizen involvement, it should also provide a revealing glimpse at the policy process itself.

Citizen Participation and
Metropolitan Fragmentation

Metropolitan fragmentation, a term referring to the number of local governments within a particular area, has been found in previous studies to be related to various measures of public policy. In general, it is assumed that fragmentation will adversely affect municipal services since, as Hawkins states, "fragmentation is said to increase the cost and to lower the quantity or quality of services."[2] Hawkins did find in his study that, although not all relationships were significant, for some services fragmentation was an important determinant of levels of spending. He concluded, "as fragmentation increases, spending decreases"[3]

53

Fragmentation has also been of interest to students of citizen participation. Generally it has been suggested that as fragmentation *decreases*, neighborhood participation programs will *increase*. Obviously, this is because of the assumption that those cities which offer greater access points to decision-making (i.e., are more fragmented) will experience fewer demands for citizen participation activities. Hawkins, among others, has concluded that less fragmented areas "may help to explain the rising demands for governmental decentralization, neighborhood autonomy, and increased citizen participation in the metropolis."[4] For the purposes of this study (and in conformance to previous research), metropolitan fragmentation was defined in two ways: (1) the absolute numbers of governmental units per area; (2) the number of governmental units per 1000 population.[5] Table 4-1 measures the following two hypotheses:

Hyp. 1: The greater the absolute number of local governmental units, the less the ranking on the citizen participation index.

Hyp. 2: The greater the relative number of local governmental units, the less the ranking on the participation scale.

As Table 4-1 indicates, the relationship between the participation index and both measures of governmental fragmentation are significant in the proposed directions. However, Tau *C* indicates the magnitude of both relationships to be relatively weak. The strength of the relationship between the absolute number of governmental units and the involvement scale was especially weak (−0.03). Even these small relationships may be further reduced when controlling for other political variables as tested below.

Table 4-1
Citizen Participation and Metropolitan Fragmentation

Participation Matrix	Number of Local Governments per Area				Number of Governmental Units per 1000			
	Less than 50	50-100	100-200	Over 200	Less than 0.20	0.20-0.50	0.50-1.0	Over 1.0
1	42.0%	48.4%	44.4%	51.0%	47.4%	40.5%	22.9%	59.1%
2	14.5	9.7	5.6	15.7	5.3	11.9	17.1	11.8
3	23.2	19.4	18.5	13.7	24.6	16.7	17.1	19.4
4	15.9	0.0	13.0	17.6	15.8	14.3	20.0	7.5
5	4.3	9.7	16.7	2.0	5.3	14.3	14.3	2.2
6	0.0	12.9	1.9	0.0	1.8	2.4	8.6	0.0
	100.0	100.0	100.0	100.0	100.0	100.0	100.0	100.0
	(N = 69)	(N = 31)	(N = 54)	(N = 51)	(N = 57)	(N = 42)	(N = 35)	(N = 93)

Significance Level = (0.01)   Significance Level = (0.01)
Tau *C* = −0.03   Tau *C* = −0.13

Citizen Participation and
Municipal Government

Two sets of hypotheses concerning the relationships between form of municipal government and citizen participation programs are closely related. One involves the relationship between citizen involvement and structural reform, the other the relationship between neighborhood organization and mayoralty strength. Each of these is explored in this section.

Essentially the same argument as that presented above, when considering the influence of class and ethnic variables on the participation index, can be made that a relationship between a city's political structure and its score on the involvement index will exist. Although it was demonstrated in Chapter 3 that the relationship between those cultural and ethnic variables which comprise the elements of the ethos theory was negligible in almost every instance, it still might be quite possible that a relationship between citizen participation and reformed political structures exists. One study has suggested, in fact, that structural elements as well as demographic variables should be considered as important elements of the ethos thesis. According to this argument, those environmental influences supposedly associated with the cultural theory apply mainly to early twentieth-century demographic characteristics of the population. These characteristics obviously have changed, however it is suggested that the product of those ethnic influences—reformed and unreformed political structures—remain intact and that cultural influences upon public policy may be filtered through these institutional variables. Thus, so the argument goes, the failure of the policy analyst to find significant relations between various demographic variables and policy output does not necessarily invalidate the cultural hypothesis. Before it is concluded that the ethos theory is of little predictive value, this argument suggests, one should examine the influence of political structure on the policy in question.[6] The attempt here is not to enter into (much less resolve) the debate over whether demographic, structural, or a combination of both measures provide the best test of the culture theory of urban politics.[7] Rather, political structure is examined below as though it may comprise an element of the ethos theory. Should such an analysis fail to demonstrate a relationship between reformism and citizen participation (or if a relationship may exist but later is found to be insignificant when controlling for other variables), the ethos theory clearly would be shown to be an inadequate predictor of this measure of urban policy. This section, then, explores these relationships.

It has been amply demonstrated in the literature that citizen involvement is antithetical to those values associated with reform political structures (such as the manager form of government, at-large elections, and nonpartisan politics). Much of this literature was reviewed in Chapter 3 and need not be repeated here. However, it is unclear as to just what relationship one should expect between reformed political structures and the movement for citizen participation. On the one hand, it is feasible to assume (as the ethos theory would predict) that citizen participation will be promoted less in more reformed cities because of the conflicting values. William Scott, for example, argues that many urban administrators are so deeply steeped in the tradition of classical administrative thought that they will be slow to adopt the new reform proposals associated with citizen participation.[8] Likewise, Adam Herbert in his discussion of the possibilities of citizen involvement in local affairs finds it "significant that many professional administrators continue to hold steadfastly to more traditional theories of administrative organization and practice."[9] Furthermore, Herbert believes that the attitude of most reform city officials is one which would not "allow uninformed, self-interest-oriented, short-sighted citizens to become obstacles to the successful and efficient functioning of government."[10] Alan Altshuler also believes that councilmen elected at-large (reform method) will oppose neighborhood participation. This is so, he says, because such a councilman "has little reason to believe that he could dominate the neighborhood politically."[11] Obviously, it would be expected that such attitudes would discourage widespread implementation of citizen participation activities in reformed municipalities.

Alternately, some have suggested that it is in those cities described as most reformed that citizen participation activities will most likely be found. On the one hand, it is argued by some that it is in those areas which in the past have emphasized standards of professionalism, neutrality, and centralization in the formulation of municipal policy and the delivery of local services that demands for citizen involvement will be the greatest. Others have suggested that officials associated with reform politics will be less threatened by citizen participation activities. Perhaps Joseph Zimmerman is most explicit when he argues that "an at-large city council [reformed] may be more sympathetic to the creation of neighborhood governments than one elected on a ward [unreformed] basis because the new system would enable the council to continue to focus its attention on city-wide issues. A ward councilman probably would oppose an institutional change that might diminish his power and influence in his area of the city."[12]

In any case, the relationship between citizen participation and political reformism as defined in the literature is ambiguous and conflicting arguments have been made concerning the likelihood of such activities being adopted by the various structures. The two alternate hypotheses (utilizing the index of structural reformism as constructed and defined in Chapter 2) which are tested by Figure 4-1, then, are as follows:

Hyp. 3: The more reformed the political structure, the greater the city's score on the participation index; or

Hyp. 4: The more reformed the political structure, the less the city's score on the involvement index.

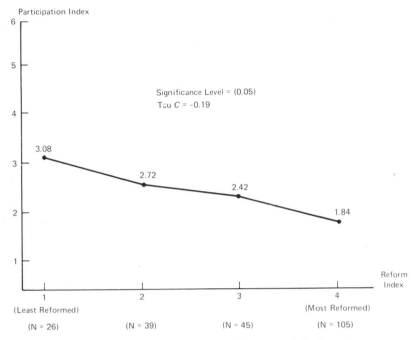

Figure 4-1. Citizen Participation and Structural Reformism.

Figure 4-1 presents the mean score of the cities in each reform category on the citizen participation index. There is a direct and consistent relationship between structural reformism and citizen involvement as revealed in Figure 4-1. The greater the city's reform score, the less its rating on the participation index ($Tau\ C = -0.19$). This relationship is especially evident when one considers simply the question of whether a city is likely to have adopted any participation program (regardless of scope or degree of intensity). Although this is not shown in Figure 4-1, over half those cities rated as most reformed have adopted no citizen participation program, whereas only about 27 percent of those cities rated the least reformed had adopted no participation program. It is evident, then, that political structure (in this case reformism) may be an important determinate in the decision to adopt or not to adopt a citizen involvement program. Although the size of this relationship may be found to diminish considerably when the influence of other factors is considered, to this point this research concurs with the conclusions of Lineberry and Fowler who found when examining several measures of municipal spending that "political institutions seem to play an important role in the political process—a role substantially independent of a city's demography."[13]

For differing reasons, it has been suggested that citizen participation will be particularly appealing to urban mayors. The thrust of this argument is that the decline of the urban machine has left the urban mayor with few (if any) vehicles for the amalgamation of sufficient political power with which to confront contemporary municipal problems and that neighborhood and citizen movements may substitute as such a mechanism.

It is clear that among its other functions the urban machine was a tremendous source of power to the nineteenth and early twentieth-century mayor. Robert Wood, for example, suggests that without the machine urban government is "devoid of most of the properties of a management enterprise" and can barely amass the power required to develop and execute public policy.[14] Also Edward Banfield, in his classic study of Chicago politics argues that the mayor can pursue a case of action only by overcoming the formal decentralization of municipal policy and that "by far the most important mechanism through which this is done is the political party or machine."[15]

It has been argued by some, then, that the new movement for citizen participation and organization might provide the mayor a substitute source of political power and thus it should be expected that proposals for a greater citizen role would be more favorably accepted by mayor-run cities. Herbert Kaufman, for one, notes the following about neighborhood groups seeking more involvement in public affairs:

Will probably discover that they get their most sympathetic hearings from chief executives, especially big city mayors. For such groups can provide the executive with counter weights to the bureaucracies: they constitute an alternative channel of information about administrative performance, reducing executive dependence on the bureaucracies. . . . Chief executives probably could not create the groups if they set out deliberately to do so, but it would be surprising if they did not eventually perceive the advantages of collaborating with them now that a variety of complaints has brought the groups spontaneously into being.[16]

Altshuler agrees with this hypothesis and, in his analysis of Model Cities legislation (which required considerable citizen participation), notes that "mayors consider the program worth lobbying for, and with some passion."[17] Also in his review of Urban Renewal legislation, James Q. Wilson finds that "many 'new-style' mayors are trying to build up new neighborhood associations and enter into relationships with old ones in order to provide themselves with a way of reaching the average voter and of commanding his support. In Boston, for example, it is an open secret that Mayor John Collins is hoping that the support and attention he has given various neighborhood associations will be reciprocated, on election day, by the support of their members for him."[18] As a final example, Zimmerman argues that "neighborhood governments may be a partial way out of the impasse [of racial polarization] for the mayor as the new power relationships inherent in such a system might enable him to avoid entirely or partially certain issues."[19] Thus the hypothesis tested below is that mayor-run, more so than manager or commission-run, cities will have adopted citizen participation programs. Also, various measures of the mayor's strength (and a scale of mayoralty strength as defined in Chapter 2) are examined to determine if there is any relationship between the mayor's legal power and the adoption of citizen participation programs. As a working hypothesis, it might be expected that the stronger mayors will be more successful in initiating citizen involvement programs (just as they should be more successful in initiating any desired legislation). These two hypotheses are tested below:

Hyp. 5: Mayor form of governments will more likely have initiated citizen participation programs than manager or commission forms.

Hyp 6: The greater the mayor's strength, the greater the likelihood of initiation of a participation program.

Table 4-2 indicates that, as hypothesized, mayor-run cities are much more likely to have adopted citizen participation programs rating higher on the scale of scope and intensity than are manager- and commission-run cities. Tau C indicates that relationship to be moderately strong (0.31). However, the proposition that stronger mayors would more likely adopt citizen participation programs was rejected.[20] In two of the three measures of mayoralty strength, the relationships were found to be insignificant and in the third measure (mayor's voting power) the relationship was significant but in the direction *opposite* that proposed. Possibly citizen involvement programs are more likely found in cities run by weak mayors (as measured by their voting power), not because these mayors are legally more capable of inacting their wishes (by definition, they are not), but because it is the legally weak mayors who are most attracted to the political power which may accrue from neighborhood organizations. Alternately, one might simply conclude that strong mayors view neighborhood programs as unnecessary competitors for power rather than as opportunities to build political organizations. In any case, the relationships between the measures of mayoralty power and participation programs were relatively weak. The most important relationship revealed by Table 4-2 is the strong tendency for mayor- (rather than commission or manager) run cities to adopt programs of neighborhood participation. This would tend to substantiate (but, of course, not prove) the proposition that mayors support participation activities in order to initiate new sources of urban political power. The implications of this are examined more fully in Chapter 7.

Citizen Participation and Urban Violence

If the basic hypotheses advanced in Chapter 1 are accurate, it would be expected that a strong positive correlation between a city's having experienced some

Table 4-2

Citizen Participation, Form of Government, and Mayoralty Strength

Participation Matrix	Form of Government		Method of Mayor's Selection		Mayor's Voting Power		
	Mayor	Manager/ Commission	Popular Election	Selected by Council	Votes on All Issues	Votes on Ties Only	No Voting Power
1	29.5%	56.7%	43.9%	55.6%	51.9%	51.3%	23.9%
2	10.3	11.3	8.4	17.5	11.6	12.8	8.7
3	23.1	17.7	21.9	14.3	18.6	17.9	26.1
4	23.1	7.1	15.5	7.9	10.1	10.3	23.9
5	10.3	5.7	8.4	3.2	6.2	7.7	10.9
6	3.8	1.4	1.9	1.6	1.6	0.0	1.4
	100.0	100.0	100.0	100.0	100.0	100.0	100.0
	(N = 78)	(N = 141)	(N = 155)	(N = 63)	(N = 129)	(N = 39)	(N = 46)

Significance Level = 0.001   Significance Level = N.S.   Significance Level = 0.05
Tau C = −0.31   Tau C = 0.18

Participation Matrix	Mayor's Veto Power			Mayor's Strength Index		
	Can Veto All Issues	Can Veto Ordinances Only	Has No Veto Power	1 (Strongest)	2	3 (Weakest)
1	40.0%	33.3%	50.4%	58.6%	42.4%	44.7%
2	4.4	16.7	12.6	3.4	8.2	17.0
3	26.7	13.3	19.3	20.7	22.4	17.0
4	17.8	20.0	10.4	13.8	15.3	11.7
5	8.9	13.3	5.9	3.4	10.6	6.4
6	2.2	3.3	1.0	0.0	1.2	3.2
	100.0	100.0	100.0	100.0	100.0	100.0
	(N = 45)	(N = 30)	(N = 135)	(N = 29)	(N = 85)	(N = 94)

Significance Level = N.S.   Significance Level = N.S.

degree of urban unrest and its score on the citizen participation index would exist. It was argued in Chapter 1 that many professional administrators, for the sake of urban tranquility, have been willing to abandon their traditional values of professionalism and efficiency and to support, instead, proposals of citizen involvement. Some have even stated that "*the most significant* citizen impact on the formulation of participation policy . . . has probably been rioting."[21] So few cities in the sample of 227 examined in this study had experienced violence of the sort which would rate at the highest categories of the violence scale developed in Chapter 2, that the violence index was simply collapsed into two categories: those experiencing no urban violence during the 1965-68 period and those experiencing some degree of unrest (this procedure, of course, still preserves the unidimensionality advantage of Guttman scaling). The hypothesis to be tested in Table 4-3 is that:

Hyp. 7: Those cities experiencing no urban violence will have initiated fewer citizen participation programs than those experiencing some degree of urban unrest.

As expected, Table 4-3 reveals a strong positive relationship between urban unrest and the participation scale. Not only are those cities having experienced some degree of urban violence more likely to have adopted some form of participation program, they are more likely to have developed programs at the upper end of the participation matrix.[22] Tau C indicates this relationship to be one of the strongest uncovered in this study (0.31). The question of whether or not participation in these programs affects a person's propensity to engage in violent and disruptive tactics cannot be answered by these data (see note 22) and will be explored in-depth in the following chapters. Here it is only demonstrated that city administrators have responded to incidents of urban violence by initiating programs encouraging citizen involvement.

At the same time, it must be noted that, whereas the basic hypothesis concerning the influence of urban unrest on the participation index was confirmed, almost half (46.0 percent) of those cities experiencing no urban violence had initiated some form of participation program. While it cannot be argued that urban unrest is not a factor involved in the decision of these cities to initiate a participation program (since they may have reacted to violence in other

Table 4-3
Citizen Participation and Urban Violence

Participation Matrix	Urban Violence Measure (1965-1968)	
	No Violence	Some Degree of Violence
1	54.0%	23.5%
2	11.4	9.8
3	20.5	17.6
4	10.8	19.6
5	2.3	23.5
6	1.1	5.9
	100.0	100.0
	(N = 176)	(N = 51)
	Significance Level = (0.001) Tau C = 0.31	

areas), still the same conclusion which was reached concerning the impact of previously considered factors seems appropriate here. Although urban violence appears to be a factor contributing to the development of neighborhood involvement organizations, it certainly cannot be concluded that such unrest (or any other single factor considered above) is the determining factor in these decisions. The following section considers the influence of one additional variable (federal grant-in-aid programs) after which the combined impact of all these political factors on the participation index is calculated.

Citizen Participation and
Federal Grants in Aid

The enormous impact which the three federally sponsored programs of Urban Renewal, OEO, and Model Cities have had on urban citizen participation was discussed in Chapter 1. A prominent scholar of citizen involvement, Alan Altshuler, was quoted in that chapter as concluding that "the whole current movement for neighborhood control was largely set in motion . . . by the Economic Opportunity Act of 1964." Suzanne Farkas has also discussed the significant impact of federal funding and guidelines on municipal decentralization and participation pressures. She states, "By the late 1960's . . . the concept of devolving authority to subunits within the cities and creating mechanisms for more citizen participation in program-planning gained favor among the federal agencies concerned with cities. There followed a surge of interest in decentralization and participation."[23]

The question to be pursued in this section is just what proportion of the citizen participation activities reported in this survey appears to be related to federally sponsored programs and what proportion appears to be independent of federal encouragement. This question is an important one not only for the academic interests of students of local politics but also for the very practical interests of those citizens and urban administrators actively involved in such programs. Presently, the Nixon administration appears to support a program which would abolish or significantly reduce the scope of these federal programs. Instead, a General and Special Revenue Sharing is being promoted which would grant more discretion over the spending of federally allocated funds to local officials. Significantly, the spending of Revenue Sharing funds requires no citizen input. It should be of particular interest, then, to determine what proportion of those cities receiving no Urban Renewal, OEO, or Model Cities funding has initiated citizen participation activities. In order to measure this relationship, a scale was developed which simply accounts for the number of federally sponsored programs each city has accepted.[24] Those cities receiving neither OEO, Model Cities, nor Urban Renewal funds were coded 0 on this scale, those involved in only one of these programs were coded 1, those accepting funds from two programs were coded 2, and those involved in all three programs were assigned a score of 3. The hypotheses tested in Figure 4-2 are as follows:

Hyp. 8: Those cities receiving either Urban Renewal, OEO, or Model Cities funds are more likely to have engaged in any form of citizen participation activities than those receiving none; and

Hyp. 9: The more of these programs with which a city is involved, the greater will be its score on the participation index.

As Figure 4-2 indicates, each of these hypotheses is confirmed. Especially noticeable is the rise in the average score of those cities receiving funds from none of these federal programs and those receiving funds from one program (1.54 to 2.07) and the rise in the average score of those receiving funds from two programs and those receiving funds from all three (2.20 to 3.55). Even more dramatic are the percentage differences between cities ranking on the varying categories of this index. Almost 72 percent of those cities receiving funds from none of these programs reported no citizen participation program. The percentage reporting no participation activity dropped to 49 percent of those receiving funds from one of these grant programs, to 44 percent of those receiving funds from two programs, and to 18 percent of those cities receiving funds from all

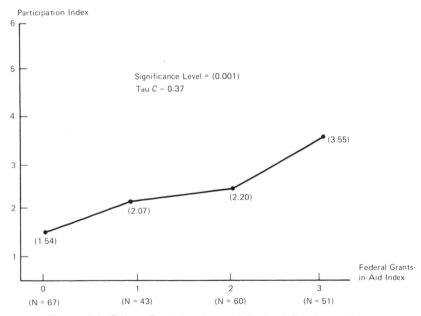

Figure 4-2. Citizen Participation and Federal Grants in Aid.

three programs. Of all those variables considered in this section, this index, measuring the extent of involvement in OEO, Model Cities, and Urban Renewal funds, clearly is one of the most important (as reflected in the Tau C value of 0.38).

As mentioned above, this relationship obviously could have serious consequences for the future of citizen participation in American cities. This is because the sources of federal funds examined above apparently are being phased out and new sources (Revenue Sharing) require no neighborhood or citizen input. As of this writing, the full implication of General and Special Revenue Sharing programs for citizen participation is, of course, only a matter of conjecture. In his message outlining his plan of Special Revenue Sharing for Urban Community Development (submitted to the Congress as the Better Communities Act), President Nixon suggested that this plan would replace programs such as Urban Renewal, Model Cities, and Neighborhood Facilities—all of which considerably contributed to the citizen participation activities in various communities.[25] However, the president assured the Congress that this act would not necessarily mean the dismantlement of programs such as Model Cities. In his message, the president stated:

One point that should be very clearly understood is that no program currently funded by categorical grants need be discontinued under the [proposed] arrangement. There is little reason to think that many cities would be motivated to dismantle their Model Cities projects under Special Revenue Sharing. . . .[26]

However confident President Nixon may be that programs such as Model Cities can survive his Revenue Sharing proposals, it is clear that some mayors and congressmen are not so certain. During the March 1973 Conference of Mayors, the nation's mayors met with the president to express their concern that Revenue Sharing would cut too deeply into such programs. Of particular concern to the mayors is the transition period between cutoffs in existing programs and the start of Special Revenue Sharing. According to Detroit Mayor Roman S. Gribbs, "As we read the budget, [assistance during the transition] is not there."[27] Also, Senators Gaylord Nelson (Democrat-Wisconsin) and Jacob Javits (Republican-New York) are concerned about the future of Community Action programs and have sponsored legislation which would provide money specifically for mayors to use in support of such programs. An aide to the senators is reported as commenting that "the administration is perpetrating a fraud when it says CAAs can survive on revenue-sharing money." Revenue Sharing money, the aide stated, is already committed to other programs, such as road-building."[28]

Although the precise impact of Revenue Sharing cannot presently be ascertained, then, it seems reasonable to conclude that citizen participation activities will not suddenly vanish. In the first place, over 28 percent of those cities receiving federal funds from none of these sources did report some degree of citizen activity (although the average score on the matrix of scope and intensity was far lower than that reported by other cities). It could be expected then, that at least about a fourth of U.S. cities will continue with citizen participation activities, regardless of alternations in federal-funding requirements. Even more important, of course, is the fact that the majority of those other cities (those receiving federal funds from one or more of these three programs) now have ongoing citizen involvement activities. Many of these, as President Nixon suggests, undoubtedly will receive financial support from Revenue Sharing funds; others will seek private sources of funding. Among those who have commented on the future of citizen participation after the discontinuance of such programs as those considered above, Henry Schmandt is worth quoting at length.

Even though the demise of OEO may be imminent and the absorption of Model Cities into the regular structure of local government a strong possibility, the participatory practices engendered by these and other urban programs of the past decade are too well established to be ignored. The chances appear slight that the more extreme forms of community control . . . will be experimented with on a broad basis in the immediate future. There are indications, nevertheless, that municipal decentralization of less extensive proportions will increase in favor with the passage of time.[29]

Despite the strong correlation between citizen participation activities and the influence of those federally funded programs currently being phased out, then, this study concurs with those who argue that citizen involvement in municipal affairs is not as temporary as the OEO and Model Cities legislation. However, based on the data presented here, it probably is reasonable to conclude that in the near future some reduction in the absolute number of cities involved in citizen participation programs is to be expected and that, of those cities continuing such programs, the intensity of citizen involvement and the scope of program activity will be noticeably reduced.

Summary: Citizen Participation
and Municipal Politics

This chapter has attempted to isolate and measure the impact of a number of political and structural variables on citizen participation activities in American cities. Some of these relationships, it was noted, are of more than just passing interest to the student of urban politics. It was suggested that the very nature of the future of participation activities may depend on the future of some of these political factors. Of course, of particular concern here is the influence of federally funded programs such as Urban Renewal, OEO, and Model Cities, which are being phased out or significantly reduced. Table 4-4 presents the zero-order coefficients, partials, and multiple correlation coefficients for the various relationships examined above.

This summary table presents relatively few deviations from those relationships presented above. It is clear that, when controlling for all other political variables, the impacts of structural fragmentation and mayoralty strength are reduced. Structural reformism appears to maintain a moderately strong effect on citizen participation (the more reformed, the less the participation index)— significant at the 0.01 level. The most important political variables associated with citizen involvement, as revealed in Table 4-4, obviously are the indices of urban violence and federal-funding (comprised of Urban Renewal, OEO, and Model Cities programs). The total percentage of variance in the participation index explained by all these variables is shown to be 0.32 (compared with 0.20 explained by the socioeconomic variables). Of course some of these relationships may be altered further when considering the combined impact of socioeconomic and political variables; however, it does appear that, when considering the nonfiscal policy of citizen participation, political factors may be at least as important as socioeconomic factors. This proposition is tested more fully in the following section.

Citizen Participation, Socioeconomic Variables, and Political Influences

It is at this point in their analysis that students of the policy process generally insert all socioeconomic and political variables *together* into a regression equation which allows each independent variable to explain what percentage of the variance in the dependent variable it can while controlling for all others. It

Table 4-4
Coefficients of Simple and Partial Correlation between Citizen Participation Index and Municipal Politics

Independent Variables	Simple r	Partial r
Scale of metropolitan fragmentation	−0.04	−0.01
Urban violence index	0.41	0.27
Index of mayoralty strength	0.05	0.06
Index of structural reformism	−0.27	−0.17
Index of federal-funding support		
(OEO, Model Cities, and Urban Renewal)	0.49	0.32
		$R = 0.560$
		$R^2 = 0.320$

usually is concluded, then, that those variables which remain significantly related to the dependent variable are the true causes (or determinants) of that variable and that the relationships which appeared important before but which are shown by these controls to be insignificant were only spurious in the first place. Although this logic is sound in one sense (that is, some spurious relationships certainly may be revealed), it is quite deceptive in another. The basic problem, as mentioned in Chapter 3, is the possibility of multicollinearity which may exist among the independent variables so that controlling for two (or more) highly correlated independent variables will probably result in depressing the significance of those which may, in fact, be important. Many methodologists have commented on this problem, however, their warnings have been paid little attention by most students of the policy process. James Noell, for example, states the problem when he says "the reasons that such [policy process] findings are probably spurious is that the independent variables in the set of socio-economic variables suffer from multicollinearity, so that when one 'controls' for variation caused by, say, industrialization, urbanization, and education to see if 'median income' has any 'independent' effect on [policy outputs] one actually controls the *valid* variation of 'median income.' "[30] Likewise, Robert Gordon warns that "when two variables are equivalent, they will both be equally valid to some degree, and controlling for one of these amounts to controlling for valid co-variation."[31] To repeat, the point which most previous students of the policy process have failed to consider when attempting to determine the relative importance of socioeconomic and political variables as predictors of urban policy is that controlling for one set of variables not only reveals possible spurious relationships, *it also depresses other relationships which may very well be direct and significant.*

Yet the policy analyst is still interested in determining which sets of factors are the most important predictors of policy outputs. The obvious question is how can this be done without masking true relationships?

Factor analysis provides such a technique. Factor analysis can be used to examine all those socioeconomic and political variables considered as independent predictors of urban policy and will extract from this total number the most important political and environmental dimensions which can then be employed in a multivariate analysis. The crucial advantage of this approach is that those dimensions (by using orthogonal rotation criteria) will be totally independent of each other.[32] Thus the problem of multicollinearity can be practically eliminated.

A factor analysis program was applied to the complete set of variables examined above.[33] The resulting rotated factor matrix is presented in Table 4-5.

As this table indicates, eight principal factors or dimensions were extracted from the original thirty-three. Together those eight factors account for almost 27 percent of the total variance of the original correlation matrix. Interestingly, of the eight factors extracted, four appear to reflect socioeconomic conditions

Table 4-5
Varimax Rotated Factor Loadings

Items:	Factors:	Population	Affluence	Federal Support	Reformed Politics	Ethnicity	Mayor's Race	Mayor's Voting Power	Urban Violence
Metropolitan type		-.082	-.129	-.550	.085	.078	-.341	.080	-.235
% Nonwhite		.232	-.010	.267	.080	-.202	.798	.065	.014
% Black		.190	-.040	.257	.074	-.221	.823	.005	.084
% Foreign born		.219	.095	-.078	-.048	.871	-.119	.196	-.048
Total foreign stock		.160	.178	-.052	-.087	.839	-.224	.228	-.077
Mean age		.034	.584	.226	.158	.661	.208	-.017	.129
% Less than 18		-.007	.837	.002	.140	-.126	.209	.148	.009
% Over 65		-.040	.237	.310	.084	.764	.125	-.185	.231
Mean school completed		.008	.946	.088	.171	.162	.055	.013	.033
% Less than 5th grade		.070	.033	.112	.008	.175	.118	.118	-.038
% More than 12th grade		-.019	.921	-.024	.137	.029	-.147	-.052	-.010
% Employed in retail		-.018	.793	.143	.156	.171	.318	-.162	.083
% Employed in white collar		-.004	.912	.061	.113	.188	.022	-.086	.021
Median income		.074	.852	-.024	.106	.209	-.165	.172	-.002
Income under $3000		-.025	.200	.282	.148	.073	.810	-.180	.123
Population		.885	.040	.158	-.027	.010	.089	.006	.104
Total revenues		.951	.021	.166	-.063	.093	.072	.042	.066
Intergovt. revenue		.846	-.000	.139	-.074	.118	.084	.051	.072
General expenditures		.940	.020	.184	-.070	.091	.093	.040	.063
Riot index, 1965		.446	.237	.062	.016	.032	.103	.129	.767
Riot index, 1966		.750	-.023	.069	.022	.035	-.002	.090	.142
Riot index, 1967		.286	-.064	.254	.037	.047	.026	.082	.550
Riot index, 1968		.491	-.091	.056	-.004	-.005	.295	-.098	.407

Form of government	-.085	.201	-.085	.566	-.054	.106	-.538	-.087
Method of mayor's selection	-.047	.074	.058	.773	.046	-.121	-.035	.002
Mayor's voting power	.154	.144	.122	-.207	.152	.076	.769	.067
Mayor's veto power	-.085	.077	.030	.830	-.031	.117	-.045	.084
Method of council selection	-.029	.310	-.059	.636	-.015	.195	-.200	-.042
Partisan politics	.060	.384	-.182	.502	-.043	-.050	.004	.398
Reform index	-.004	.065	.081	.760	.112	.094	.490	.100
Model cities funds	.365	.014	.640	-.002	-.012	.032	.081	.081
OEO funds	.104	-.026	.779	-.025	.020	.270	.011	.056
Urban renewal funds	.104	.082	.769	.002	.157	.153	.103	-.027
Eigenvalues:	8.035	6.457	4.043	2.891	2.208	1.524	1.408	1.016
Percentage of Total Variance:	0.223	0.199	0.112	0.081	0.061	0.042	0.040	0.028
Cumulative % of Total Variance:	0.223	0.402	0.514	0.595	0.656	0.698	0.738	0.766

(as examined in Chapter 3) and four appear to represent those political conditions discussed in this chapter.

Factor I (accounting for 22 percent of the variance) appears to differentiate between municipalities on the basis of population and absolute expenditures. Loading high on this dimension are the variables of population size, total revenues, and total general expenditures. Also loading relatively strong on this dimension are the measures of riot intensity (although these also form their own independent dimension). This factor, then, appears to be basically an indicator of *population.*

Factor II (accounting for 18 percent of the variance) is obviously a measure of *metropolitan affluence.* Loading high on this factor are such variables as median school years completed, proportion employed in white-collar occupations, and median income.

Factor III (which accounts for 11 percent of the variance) is an indicator of the *federal-funding support* for citizen participation activities. Loading high on this dimension are the indicators of whether or not a city received OEO, Model Cities, or Urban Renewal funds.

Factor IV (accounting for 8 percent of the variance) differentiates between characteristics of local governmental structure. This dimension is comprised of such measures as form of government (mayor or commission), mayor's veto power, selection of councilmen, and so forth. Specifically, the structural characteristics of those cities ranking high on this dimension are those which:

1. Are less likely to have a mayor form of government
2. Are less likely to elect the chief executive by popular vote (that is, he is more likely to be selected by the council)
3. Are less likely to allow the mayor a strong (if any) veto power
4. Are less likely to elect councilmen by ward processes
5. Are less likely to have adopted partisan (party ballot) election methods
6. Are more likely to have weak mayors

This dimension is simply labeled *reformed politics*, since it distinguishes between those variables generally associated with the reform package of government.

Factor V (explaining 6 percent of the variance) distinguishes between the *ethnic characteristics* of the various cities. Loading high on this factor are those variables measuring percentage foreign born, total foreign stock, and median age.

Factor VI (explaining 4 percent of the variance) is a reflection of the *racial composition* of the various cities. Such variables as percentage black, percentage nonwhite, percentage with less than fifth grade education, and percentage with income under $3,000, load high on this dimension.

Factor VII (accounting for 4 percent of the total variance) is a curious dimension since it would intuitively seem that the single variable loading high on this measure (mayor's voting strength) would belong with those other measures of mayoralty structure which loaded high on Factor IV. Nevertheless, this variable does form its own dimension, independent of all others, which is labeled *mayoralty voting strength.*

Finally, accounting for 3 percent of the variance, Factor VIII obviously is a measure of the extent of *urban violence.* Loading high on this dimension are the several indices of urban unrest which were described above.

This description of the important dimensions which were extracted from this matrix is purposefully brief because the emphasis here is not just the determination of which of these variables seem to cluster together, reflecting separate and independent dimensions of the urban political and social environment. Although this may be of interest to some, the primary purpose of this use of factor analysis is the construction of uncorrelated independent predictors of citizen participation activities. In effect, each of these factors, which again are uncorrelated with one another, may be treated as a variable upon which every city is ranked (by factor scores). Thus a determination of which of these socioeconomic and political environments are most directly (one might even say causally) related to the participation matrix, avoiding the problem of multicollinearity, is now possible. Table 4-6 presents the correlation coefficients between each factor and the index of citizen participation.

The coefficients presented in Table 4-6 generally tend to confirm and reinforce those relationships noted earlier. Of the four dimensions reflecting environmental influences, two (affluence and ethnicity) failed to meet the 0.05 criteria of significance. The cities' racial composition displayed a significant

Table 4-6
Citizen Participation and Environmental and Political Dimensions

Dimensions	Correlation and Beta Coefficients[a]	Significance
Population	0.20	0.002
Affluence	−0.02	N.S.
Federal support	0.41	0.001
Reformed politics	−0.07	N.S.
Ethnicity	0.06	N.S.
Race	0.13	0.02
Mayor's voting power (Negatively Measured)	0.13	0.02
Urban violence	0.16	0.008
		$R = 0.527$
		$R^2 = 0.278$

[a]Since each factor is completely independent of the other, the zero-order correlation coefficients, partials, and betas are all equivalent.

relationship with the participation index (the greater the proportion black, the higher the score on the involvement scale); and, as mentioned in Chapter 3, population emerges as the most important environmental determinant of citizen participation. This would appear to suggest that citizen involvement is not just a movement catering to the urban black community (although the proportion black obviously is a significant influence). More important, it seems, citizen participation is a response to the more general phenomenon of city size. Robert Dahl suggests that political participation in the large metropolis has become largely a frustrating and symbolic experience.[34] A reasonable hypothesis which might be advanced is that as city size reaches and surpasses a point where participation becomes a token (or, in Dahl's term, "symbolic") gesture, citizens (of all racial and ethnic groups) seek more meaningful channels by which they may formulate and express their political desires. The classical theory of democracy, it will be recalled, argues that participation (treated as the causal variable) is to be valued because of the educational benefits and psychological effects (treated as the dependent variables) which it may have for the individual. To the extent possible, these relationships are treated in Chapters 5 and 6. Here, it is suggested that the psychological effects of what is felt to be meaningless participation in mass society (anomie, distrust, alienation, isolation, etc.[35]) may cause individuals to seek more direct means of political expression. Such a proposition is at least more compatible with the data presented here than the theory of ethnic or cultural determinism. The implications of these findings for the ethos theory are explored more fully in the concluding section of this chapter.

Table 4-6 confirms earlier findings that those variables treated as measures of political differentiations among American cities are, by far, the most important determinants of citizen participation activities. As the Beta measures indicate, indices of urban violence and mayoralty strength are roughly equivalent in a causal sense. Interestingly, the negative relationship between mayoralty strength (as reflected in their voting powers) and the participation index noted earlier is maintained. Thus weak mayor systems are more likely to adopt citizen participation activities than strong mayor cities. Again, it is suggested that weak mayors may desire the organizational strength which neighborhood groups make possible and that strong mayors may fear their competition. By far the most important dimension of all is that measuring federal support (by acceptance of OEO, Model Cities, or Urban Renewal grants) of citizen participation activities. This relationship is strong, regardless of city size, levels of violence, or any other dimension examined in Table 4-6. The implications of these relationships are discussed more fully in the concluding section.

Conclusion: Citizen Participation, Political Culture, and the Urban Policy Process

The primary purpose of these last two chapters has been to explain the varieties of citizen participation activities throughout the American cities. One theory, which some have suggested should account for this variation, is the cultural or ethos theory. However, this thesis was found to be of almost no predictive value. Others have argued that citizen participation is mainly associated with black demands for urban reform, however, this explanation also was found to account for only a small proportion of the variance in the participation matrix. This analysis did show that the decision to adopt a program of citizen involvement (and if so which sort) like most policy decisions cannot be explained by a single factor (such as cultural variety, or racial influences, etc.). Rather, a number of factors impinge upon that decision. In this case, the most important of these was found to be federal encouragement and requirement by way of OEO, Model Cities, and Urban Renewal grants. Second in importance was found to be city size. The larger the city, the higher its score on the participation index. Next in importance is the degree of urban violence experienced by each city. This is followed in importance by the measure of mayoralty strength and proportion black. These findings have significant implications for the cultural theory of urban politics, the urban policy-process model, and the very future of citizen participation. This concluding section discusses each of these in turn.

It is apparent, in the first place, that the cultural theory of urban politics is of almost no explanatory value when considering the policy of citizen participation. This is especially important since, as documented above, many have suggested that the decision to establish or not to establish programs of citizen involvement should be a particularly appropriate test of such a theory. The factor analysis routine generated three dimensions which very closely approximated the various elements of the ethos theory. One (and perhaps the most important) was labeled "ethnicity," another was labeled "affluence" (or class), and the third was found to represent "reformed" political structures (themselves supposedly a product of the cultural environment). One of the most important finds of these two chapters is that *in each case*, the relationships of these dimensions to the citizen participation index was found to be insignificant. These findings add further weight to the conclusion of those such as Wolfinger and Field who observed that "the ethos theory is irrelevant to the South, inapplicable to the West, and fares badly in the Northeast."[36] Regardless of whatever value it may once have had, the mounting evidence indicates that a cultural thesis of politics is no longer applicable to urban America.

These findings also have important implications for the urban policy-process model. As discussed in Chapter 3, many scholars using that model have concluded that municipal politics appear to be less important in determining levels of policy output than do environmental measures. Examining this literature, Hawkins felt warranted in concluding that "the importance of socioeconomic environments in policy explanation has raised serious doubts about the relevance of many variables that political scientists had earlier valued for their ability to explain public policy. The burden of proof has now shifted to those who would maintain that system variables are in themselves sufficient for explaining policy outputs."[37] A number of flaws in the application of this model to urban politics were discussed above, including the problem of multicollinearity of independent predictive variables. However, the most important omission of previous studies, it was argued, was their failure to include in their list of policy outputs nonfiscal measures of public policy. This study has examined one such nonfiscal policy and found that those variables generally treated as political measures were actually more important than socioeconomic measures. These findings are also of interest to the student of the policy process because of their implications for leadership influence in that process. Observers of the policy process are just beginning to explore the effects of leadership style, personality, and characteristics on policy outputs.[38] One of the more interesting relationships revealed above was that between mayoralty strength and the participation index (the weaker the mayor, the greater the city's score on the involvement scale). A number of possible explanations for that (negative) relationship were offered above, and it is only suggested here that these findings indicate that the whole area of leadership influence upon public policy may indeed warrant more in-depth investigation.

Also, from the perspective of the urban policy process, this study has demonstrated the complexity of that model. Even when considering this single policy—citizen participation activities—it was found that no single explanation alone could adequately account for the variations in the policy. In a more general sense, it seems reasonable to conclude, as have others, that any theory of urban policy-making based on a single gross phenomenon (whether it be called ethos or reformism or whatever) is destined to be a simplistic and inadequate model of the policy process.[39] This is not meant to suggest that an attempt to construct a satisfactory model of a single policy, or even of the entire policy process, would be impossible; it simply means that the process of policy-making is very complicated and that such a model will have to be as intricate as the process it attempts to explain.[40]

Finally, these findings may have significant implications for the future of citizen participation activities in American cities. This is especially true, of course, concerning the tremendous impact which federal support has had upon the initiation of these programs. Of all those variables examined, federal support was by far the most important (twice as important, in fact, as the second most powerful predictor of the participation index—population). As was mentioned above, this relationship could be of crucial importance to the future of citizen participation since the Nixon administration is now abolishing or drastically altering these very programs. In their place, a program of General Revenue Sharing is proposed which does *not* require any form of citizen or neighborhood involvement. The immediate effect of this policy on citizen participation activities, of course, can only be speculated upon. However, the data presented above suggest the following: (1) there will be a reduction in the absolute number of citizen participation activities; (2) however, at least in the short run, the programs will *not* be totally abolished from the urban scene—it was noted above that 28 percent of those cities receiving no federal funds reported some form of participation activity; and (3) those programs remaining will average a lower score on the involvement index (that is intensity of citizen participation and scope of program activity will be less) than what is currently observed. One would expect, also, that those other characteristics of citizen participation activities illustrated in Table 4-6 would be accentuated. That is, citizen involvement in the future will more than likely be *more* associated with larger cities, legally weak mayors, larger proportions of blacks, and levels of urban violence than at present. In summary, the data presented here leave little doubt but that citizen participation activities of the future will be less numerous and intense than at present, but that it would be inappropriate to predict a total dismantlement of those programs now in operation.

This chapter, then, using as its guide the policy-process model, has attempted to assess the political and environmental determinants of the citizen participation movement. Important flaws in previous applications of the process were revealed and avoided in this analysis. As a result, a considerable amount of the variance in the participation policies of American cities was explained. Nevertheless, this presentation (because of the lack of information) also slighted important elements of that model. In particular, it is suggested that more appropriate measures of public opinion and leadership attitudes and style might provide even more fruitful results. Rough measures of public opinion (such as levels of urban unrest and proportion black) and leadership characteristics (such as mayoralty strength) were employed—and found to be significant—in this analysis. However, it must be admitted that these hardly substitute for more sophisticated measures of these factors which could be provided by public opinion surveys and in-depth leadership studies. Unfortunately, it is not always feasible to conduct such surveys (as was the case here) and the researcher simply must employ what data is available. It is only suggested here that future attempts to analyze citizen participation (or any other public policy) might well benefit from more accurate assessments of these variables.

Even more important, of course, the analysis presented so far has not attempted to account for the impact of citizen participation policy. This aspect of the process model is explored in Chapters 5 and 6.

5

Participant Motives and Descriptive Characteristics

To this point, this study has presented a macrolevel, or aggregate, analysis of citizen participation in American cities. Such an approach was appropriate for the type of questions pursued—the determination of the sociopolitical environments most conducive to citizen involvement activities. Of equal importance is the type of information which can be supplied only by microlevel, or in-depth, analyses of citizen participation programs. Such information includes the descriptive representativeness (defined below) of the various program-types, the motives and goals of participants, and especially the impact of participation on the various attitudes and opinions of the participants and the neighborhood as a whole. These questions are pursued in this and the following chapter.

The impact or outcome of participation on the citizen is of particular importance in the following analysis. Although policy impact is an integral part of the entire policy process, the problems involved in an analysis of impact are undoubtedly much more complex than those associated with any other phase of the process, and consequently, it is one of the least explored aspects of the entire policy process. As Charles O. Jones has commented, "evaluation of policy is one of the least explored functional activities in the policy process."[1] Jones goes on to list the kinds of data required for a complete analysis of policy and concludes: "Imagine the difficulties one would encounter in obtaining these types of information. In order to compile such data for policies at any one level of government, it would be necessary to establish a separate agency."[2] Ronald Weber and William Shaffer have noted, more specifically, that when the policy goal is clearly stated (such as eradication of disease), the measurement and evaluation of outcome is relatively simple. However, when the policy goal is more elusive (such as quality education), Weber and Shaffer warn that "the measurement of the policy outcome is extremely difficult."[3] As the introductory chapter made clear, the goals of citizen participation are very ambiguous and, to some extent, even contradictory. For some, citizen participation is valued because of its supposed effect on citizen trust and confidence, for others it is hoped that citizen participation will improve the delivery of goods and services. Still others may expect citizen involvement to increase the political awareness and consciousness of those previously ignored by the decision-making process. Regardless of these measurement problems, this chapter and the one which follows attempt to evaluate the impact of citizen participation on a number of key participant attitudes and opinions. To do so, of course, required an extensive survey of the attitudes of those citizens involved in these various programs. As discussed in Chapter 2, 396 participants involved in twenty-six ongoing programs in four states and six metropolitan areas were selected for inclusion in this analysis. Before reviewing these findings, the remainder of this section briefly discusses the significance of such a presentation.

An examination of citizen involvement programs from the perspective of neighborhood residents participating in these programs is of interest for several reasons. There simply is very little known about the characteristics, opinions, motives, and goals of citizen participants in neighborhood organizations. Comparatively, a great deal has been written about citizen involvement from the perspective of the professional administrator.[4] That which is known about resident reaction to participation activities has been presented in an interpreted form either by academicians,[5] or by members of program staffs.[6] A typical evaluation of this sort is illustrated by Ralph Kramer's statement that, "with respect to the attitudes and the economic conditions of the poor, *those closest to the program staff* ... were in agreement that the program helped [only] a very small number. ... "[7] An examination of participant opinions, then, should test several widely-held (but unproven) assumptions concerning the attitudes, goals, and behavior of those who do participate in such neighborhood groups. Many observers believe, for example, that blacks who participate in neighborhood programs are mainly pursuing a policy of total racial separation. Henry Schmandt has commented that, among other objections to citizen participation is the criticism "that neighborhood control would promote racial separation."[8] Others have commented on the degree of internal conflict which the programs could be expected to generate.[9] Some have discussed the goals which participants in the varying programs could be expected to pursue.[10] A number of scholars are concerned with the degree of allegiance these participants will feel toward public officials,[11] and others are concerned with the representativeness of these programs.[12] The point is, these sorts of basic questions can be answered only from surveys of the attitudes of citizens participating in such programs, and such a perspective has yet to be presented.

Beyond providing basic information of this sort, it has been argued that an analysis of the characteristics and attitudes of those citizens associated with the various program types is an extremely important aspect of the overall attempt to evaluate the success or failure of these programs. On the one hand, some have argued that an analysis of the *descriptive characteristics* of participants, and the comparison of these with constituent characteristics, may provide important clues to the potential effectiveness and ultimate success of the program. For any group to be effective, argues Neil Gilbert, the social and demographic characteristics of its members must display a certain degree of congruency with those of its constituency. Considering OEO-funded neighborhood participation programs in particular, Gilbert says, "Because the poor are a diverse group, achievement of congruent membership is particularly relevant. ... Solidarity may be weakened if a disproportionate number of citizen participants are not of the poor population, such as the Negro, the working class, or the elderly."[13] Basically, Gilbert argues that a strong positive psychological identification by a constituency to an organization which proposes to represent that group is necessary if that organization is to succeed, and that such an identification is possible only when a certain degree of congruency between the constituents and the representatives exist.

In addition to this sort of analysis, of course, evaluations by the citizens themselves will be examined. Citizen input, as David A. Caputo has argued, should be considered an integral aspect of the process of evaluating any public policy or program and should be encouraged "throughout the evaluative process."[14] As yet, however, only evaluations of participation programs by public officials are available.[15] Since, as suggested in Chapter 1, success or failure of a program of neighborhood participation is often defined in terms of alterations in citizen attitudes and perceptions, it is particularly crucial to assess citizen opinions when evaluating citizen participation programs. In the analysis which follows, the success or failure of these programs, from the perspective of the neighborhood participant, is assessed. It is especially important that the attitudes of all those involved in citizen participation activities (including, of course, the citizen) be presented before a final evaluation is reached because, as others have observed, it is very possible that the same citizen involvement activity may be rated as unsatisfactory by one constituency (such as citizens) and as satisfactory by another (such as public officials). Melvin Mogulof, for example, believes that "there is a strong possibility that different patterns of citizen participation may be more or less effective in achieving certain kinds of goals."[16] A program may achieve its goal of increasing citizen trust (and thus presumably rated satisfactorily by city officials) but may fail to measurably improve the quality or delivery of municipal services (and be rated low by neighborhood participants). This analysis, then, seeks to determine if the achievement of one goal by a particular program-type excludes the achievement of others or if those programs rated high on one measure of goal achievement also rank high on other evaluative measures. If differences of this sort do exist and are exposed by this study, decisionmakers and interested citizens would be provided with a more rational basis for the selection of one program-type over another.

At an even broader theoretical level, such an analysis is consistent with the traditional concern of political scientists with the impact of structural differences on citizen behavior. At the urban level, it has been found that various structural arrangements may affect voting turnout,[17] tax policies,[18] urban renewal success,[19] and the incidence of race riots.[20] In a recent article, Peter Eisinger demonstrates a relationship between various reformed political structures (defined in a manner similar to that presented in Chapter 2 of this study) and protest behavior.[21] In short, students of political science have long been interested in exploring the linkages between political structure and political behavior. Noting this concern, Eisinger states, "The manner in which individuals and groups in the political system behave, then, is not simply a function of the resources they command but of the openings, weak spots, barriers, and resources of the political system itself. There is, in this sense, interaction, or linkage, between the environment understood in terms of the notion of a structure of political opportunities, and political behavior."[22] This analysis, then, attempts to determine what, if any, effect the various structural arrangements examined in this study may have on political attitudes and behavior.

Thus it is suggested that information collected from citizens participating in neighborhood organizations will supply hard evidence to support (or refute) a number of basic assumptions which have been offered concerning the motives and attitudes of such citizens. This chapter is concerned with the attitudinal and demographic characteristics of citizen participants; the manner in which these characteristics vary by program type; and the consequences of these characteristics for program activities and success. Chapter 6 then explores the effect (or outcome) of participation on the individual participant. Specifically, the following three questions are pursued in this chapter: what are the demographic and attitudinal characteristics of program participants; how do these characteristics vary by program type; and what are the consequences of these characteristics for program operations? In each case, the primary independent variable to be examined is the matrix of program scope and intensity, discussed below.

The Independent Variable

In the previous two chapters a citizen participation matrix of intensity and scope was employed as the *dependent* variable; in this and the following chapter, in an attempt to gauge the effect of the various programs, a similar scale is used as the *independent* variable. It will be recalled from Chapter 2 that the nature of the programs visited suggested an index of five scale-scores varying from those in which citizen participation was least intense and program scope was most narrowly focused (coded 1) to those in which participation was most intense and the scope of program coverage was the broadest (coded 5). Table 5-1 presents the distribution of the twenty-six programs along this index.

As Table 5-1 indicates, approximately 13 percent of the sample was involved in programs rated at the lowest end of the spectrum and 19 percent was involved in programs ranked at the highest scale value. The mean score of all participants in this matrix is shown to be 3.19. The following section examines the motives and goals of those participating in these programs.

Citizen Participation and Attitudinal Variables

Given the attention the topic has received in the citizen participation literature, it is surprising that so few studies have attempted to empirically examine the

Table 5-1
The Citizen Participation Index of Programs Visited

Citizen Participation Index	Number of Citizens	Percentage of Total	Cumulative Percentage of Total
1 (Least intensive involvement and most narrowly focused)	51	12.7%	12.7%
2	75	19.0	31.6
3	95	24.1	55.7
4	100	25.3	81.0
5 (Most intensive involvement and broadest program coverage)	75	19.0	100.0
	N = 396	100.0%	

Mean = 3.19
Median = 3.26

motives and goals of those residents who participate in programs of neighborhood involvement. Alan Altshuler has suggested that community officials are most likely to judge these programs from the perspective of the group's possible impact on the community's racial tensions and on the officials' own political prospects. One of the most potent arguments against citizen participation, Altshuler finds, is the fear of many whites that "community control would be a step toward racial separation" and therefore would "intensify, rather than alleviate, social friction."[23] Also, Schmandt finds that the critics of citizen participation "charge that [it] would promote racial separation."[24] Furthermore Altshuler says, local politicians "are likely to have even greater immediate interest in whether particular steps in the direction of [citizen participation and neighborhood government] will reduce or heighten racial tensions, win grudging acceptance from or outrage from the public bureaucracy, improve or imperil their own reelection prospects"[25] Thus it should be expected that those groups whose members are less motivated by such goals as neighborhood separation and/or political confrontation and are more concerned with such goals as community service, education, and employment are more likely in the future to receive favorable support from city hall. It is possible, in addition, that motives and goals might significantly affect an individual's own evaluation of the success of the program. It is conceivable, for example, that one whose motive for participation involves the active promotion of significant social and/or political changes may find participation a much more frustrating and useless experience than one whose goals are more moderate. Having been commissioned to present the views of the neighborhood participants of a Philadelphia Model Cities program, whose goal the citizens established as a "struggle to . . . create a new balance of power between ourselves and City Hall," Sherry Arnstein relates the many frustrating and agonizing experiences of those participants. Such a group, she finds, "must be prepared to fight each frustrating step of the way." Furthermore, she finds, such experiences are likely to affect the citizens' evaluation of the program. Again, writing for the group, Arnstein states, "Our experiences with unsympathetic and antagonistic officials . . . have convinced us that Model Cities is designed to deceive the community by pacifying our minds, our spirit, and our ambitions."[26] The proposition that a participant's goals and motives may affect his program evaluation is tested in the following section. Here it is determined whether these motives vary by program type.

A few attempts at program classification, by goal orientation, are available. James Vanecko classified Community Action Agencies in fifty cities according to the degree to which they emphasized four objectives: (1) education; (2) social service; (3) employment; (4) community organization and mobilization.[27] Likewise, Kenneth Clark and Jeannette Hopkins classified fifty-one CAAs according to the degree to which they stressed services, community organization, and community action.[28]

However, very few studies have attempted to assess the motives and goal orientations of individual *participants*. There is at present almost no information concerning the degree to which neighborhood participants may view these programs as means to neighborhood separation and control, tactics of political opposition and reform, opportunities to improve the delivery of neighborhood goods and services, and so forth. One study which has focused specifically on the individual motives of neighborhood participants is Gilbert's survey of CAA board members in Pittsburgh. Interestingly, he found in his study that there was a rather wide discrepancy in the board members' perception of their own motives but, most significantly, only a very small proportion interpreted their role as one of generating power and influence.[29] The vast majority of those in Gilbert's survey viewed their role as one of either facilitating communications between the neighborhood and governmental agencies (especially the community welfare agency) or as a mechanism for educating the neighborhood.[30]

In attempting to gauge the motives and goal orientations of those participating in the twenty-six programs included in this study, each participant was asked to respond to two questions. The first asked the respondent directly if he believed the "various racial and ethnic groups should work together to solve their own problems or should these groups separate their institutions and control their own affairs." This obviously should determine the extent to which blacks (and whites) in the sample favor racial separation. However, as Altshuler points out, a fear of racial and ethnic separation is not the only concern of local officials. They also are likely to be suspicious of those groups presenting a possible political threat. Thus, in addition to the question on racial separation, the survey asked each participant to indicate, in his own words, his reasons for participating. No preconceived response set was provided for this question; rather, the respondent was encouraged to list as many motives and goals as he felt appropriate. Based primarily on the few studies mentioned above, the hypotheses to be tested in Tables 5-2 and 5-3 are the following:

Hyp. 1: Black participants are more likely than whites to favor racial and ethnic separation.

Hyp. 2: The majority of participants will not view their participation as a vehicle for direct political action, confrontation, or influence.

Surprisingly, given the degree to which such observers as Altshuler and Schmandt believe whites fear a black motive of racial separation, Table 5-2 indicates that a *lesser* proportion of blacks than whites in this sample favored a racial separation of institutions and social activities. In fact, the most important relationship revealed in Table 5-2 is that almost the total sample (both black and white) opposed racial and/or ethnic separation. The available evidence (including Gilbert's study), then, indicates that participation programs are likely to attract those committed to racial and ethnic *integration* rather than separation and that concerns to the contrary are unwarranted. Still, of course, a substantial portion of those participants might view participation as a means of direct political action and confrontation (which Altshuler also finds offensive to the power structure). This possibility is examined in Table 5-3.

Most of the categories in Table 5-3 are self-explanatory. As would be expected from an open-ended question, it was found that a great many individuals could not identify specific motivations or reasons for participation but reported, instead, to be concerned simply with general neighborhood and community improvement. Examples of responses so coded include the following: "I am concerned about my neighborhood and want to share my opinions and time with other concerned people for a better neighborhood"; "I am concerned for the physical and social well-being of a neighborhood verging

Table 5-2
Separation Attitudes by Race

Should the Various Racial and Ethnic Groups Separate their Institutions and Control their own Affairs?	Black Response	White Response
Yes	6.4%	6.3%
Uncertain	2.6	6.7
No	91.0	87.0
Total N =	78	300

Table 5-3
Summary of Motives for Participation

Motives:	First Response	Second Response	Third Response
1) Fellowship—getting acquainted with neighbors	3.0%	5.4%	33.3%
2) Concern with general neighborhood improvement	63.6	27.0	22.2
3) Property owner—concern with land values	14.5	12.2	11.1
4) Various specific social concerns—community safety, employment, education child care, etc.	1.2	13.6	0.0
5) Organize for political power, protest, or confrontation	10.9	27.0	22.2
6) Community information and education	5.2	12.2	11.1
7) Encourage participation in Politics—voter registration	1.5	2.7	0.0

on deterioration"; "I am concerned for the quality of community life and also want to stop [the] exodus of middle class whites to [the] suburbs"; and "I believe strongly in the obligation of each person to contribute whatever talents they have to the improvement of the community in which they live—and I believe this is *my* best way."

Thus, as Table 5-3 indicates, the majority (63.6 percent) of the *first* motives mentioned for participation in these programs involved a general interest in community betterment and improvement. The next most often recorded first response was a concern with decreasing property values (14.5 percent) and the hope that participation in such an organization could halt this trend. Interestingly, and in concurrence with Gilbert's findings, only about 11 percent of this group indicated as its first motive for participation a desire to organize for political protest and influence. However, of those who volunteered second and third reasons for participating, this picture is dramatically altered. As indicated in Table 5-3, the proportion reporting general community improvement as a second or third motive is reduced significantly, whereas a corresponding rise in the proportion reporting a desire for political influence is recorded (still, however, only about a fourth of those listing a second or third motive mentioned active political concerns). In summary, then, these findings generally agree with those of scholars such as Clark and Hopkins who have found that such groups are not organized principally for political action. Rather, those in this study are more concerned with general neighborhood problems such as property values, the flight to the suburbs, and neighborhood safety. It was noted that of those who gave second and third motives, the proportion interested in political action increased significantly, however, those so responding still comprised only a relatively small percentage of the total.

An interesting question arises as to whether the nature of the program itself attracts participants with differing goals and motives. That is, do the motives and goals of those participating in programs rated at the upper end of the program index measurably differ from those participating in other programs? In the absence of any previous work in this area, it is assumed that those programs at the upper end of the scope and intensity index will offer more opportunities for political influence and therefore will attract those more concerned with political action. Specifically, the hypothesis to be tested in Table 5-4 is:

Hyp. 3: The greater the program's score on the participation index, the greater the proportion of participants who will record political action and protest as a motive for participation.

Table 5-4 generally confirms this hypothesis. As is indicated in that table, less than 10 percent of those participating in those programs ranked 1, 2, or 3 on

Table 5-4
Summary of Participant Motives by Program Type

Motives	Index Scores				
	1	2	3	4	5
1) Fellowship–getting acquainted with neighbors	0.0%	5.0%	5.0%	7.0%	0.0%
2) Concern with general neighborhood improvement	79.0	51.0	58.0	44.0	60.0
3) Property owner–concern with land values	12.0	25.0	19.0	9.0	5.0
4) Various specific social concerns–community safety, employment, education, child care, etc.	0.0	5.0	3.0	5.0	0.0
5) Organize for political power, protest, or confrontation	4.0	8.0	7.0	22.0	23.0
6) Community information and education	0.0	6.0	5.0	10.0	7.0
7) Encourage participation in politics–voter registration	0.0	0.0	0.0	3.0	5.0
N =	48	83	94	109	92

Note: Total N is greater than 396 because all three responses to the question of motive for each participant are summarized in this table.

this index cited political activism, protest, or influence as their first, second, or third motive for participation; whereas about a fourth of those participating in those programs ranked 4 and 5 so responded. If the political motivations and expectations of participants is a factor in future decisions to support citizen involvement programs (as Altshuler has suggested) this study would again concur with the conclusion of Schmandt (and others) who suggests that, although programs of citizen participation are too well entrenched to be completely eliminated, "the chance appears slight that the more extreme forms of community participation" will be continued.[31] Still, one must conclude from the data which is available that even in the more extreme program-types, only a small proportion of participants view their role in terms of political opposition or agitation. Interesting, also, is the effect of participation motives and goals upon program evaluations. The following section examines this relationship.

**Participant Motives and Evaluation
of Success**

Many observers have speculated upon the motives of those neighborhood residents participating in decentralization programs and, as noted above, some have attempted to empirically assess these goals. However, only a very few have systematically explored the link between such expectations and evaluations of program success. That is, although participant motives are often considered significant in the literature of citizen participation, or, for that matter, any process of representation, very few have demonstrated the actual impact of these attitudinal characteristics.

However, there is some evidence to support the assumption that those whose primary motive of participation is political mobilization or confrontation will be less satisfied with program results than those whose motives center around social service and welfare concerns. Arnstein's description of the frustrating experiences of the Philadelphia CAA was presented above. Also, Vanecko, who classified fifty CAAs according to the degree to which they emphasized education, social service, employment, and community organization and mobilization, concluded that "the effective community action program is one . . . which has neighborhood centers uninvolved in militant activities, and which does not spend time pressing specific demands on other institutions."[32] Likewise, Kramer in his study of five CAAs found those agencies whose goal was the redistribution of political power experienced more internal "dissensus," and reached "no congruence on values or interests." These organizations, he concluded, "fell far short of their goal [political mobilization]."[33]

In attempting to determine the participants' satisfaction with program results, each respondent was asked to: (1) rate the *overall* success of the program in achieving its goals and objectives; and (2) to list three most important goals of each program (as defined by each participant) and rate the program's success in achieving each. Thus four measures of program satisfaction were solicited. In the determination of whether or not goal orientation affected an individual's evaluation of success, the respondents simply were divided into those who mentioned as an important motivation political change, activism, confrontation, or mobilization and those who mentioned only social service and welfare goals. Based on previous studies, it is expected that those whose motive was some form of political action would be less satisfied with program results than those stressing service motives. The hypothesis tested in Table 5-5, then, is:

Hyp. 4: Those individuals whose motive for participation was political action- (rather than welfare and service) oriented are more likely to be dissatisfied with the program results than other participants.

As coded, a positive correlation coefficient indicated agreement with the anticipated relationship. Table 5-5 indicates that each of these measures of program and goal satisfaction are in the expected direction (those whose motives were welfare- and service-oriented were more likely to be satisfied with the program), however, only one was found to be statistically significant. Contrary, then, to the predicted relationship, this research found that when each participant was asked to evaluate for himself the results of each program, his motive for participation was of very little significance.

In summary, these two sections have explored the relationship between the participation index, participant attitudinal variables, and program success (as evaluated by each participant). It was found that most of those participating in these programs were not motivated by desires of racial separation or even concerns of political action or confrontation. However, it was found that a

Table 5-5
Program Satisfaction by Participation Motive[a]

| Motive | Measures of Satisfaction | | | |
	Overall Satisfaction	Satisfaction with Goal 1	Satisfaction with Goal 2	Satisfaction with Goal 3
Political Action/ Other	0.10[b]	0.06[a]	0.09[a]	0.02[a]

[a]Significance Level = Not Significant
[b]Significance Level = 0.05

[a]As discussed in Chapter 2, the samples used for this portion of the study were not drawn by a strict process of randomization. Therefore, the tests of significance used in this and following tables appearing in Chapters 5 and 6, are meant only to be suggestive of possible patterns in the population and are not to be interpreted as definitive.

disproportionate share of those who were so motivated were participating in those programs rated at the upper end of the program. This would indicate, once again, that if a reduction in citizen participation programs is to be expected, those most likely to be phased out are those rated at the higher levels of programs scope and participant intensity. It has not yet been determined whether those programs assigned higher scale values are more effective in terms of increasing participant efficacy, improving trust, or improving the delivery of services. These concerns are explored in Chapter 6, and a final evaluation of the implications of the results reported here is presented following that analysis. In addition, it was found that the motives of individual participants (defined as those favoring and those not supporting goals of political action) had almost no effect on participant evaluations of program success. The following section explores the relationships between programs operations, organization, and participant demographic variables.

Citizen Participation and Descriptive Characteristics

It is common for observers of political behavior to note a gap between the demographic characteristics of representatives and those they represent.[34] Representatives normally display higher socioeconomic characteristics than their constituents. Thus it should not be surprising to find that those participating in these twenty-six neighborhood programs display characteristics noticeably different from the rest of their neighborhoods. This relationship is examined below, however, the central question pursued in this section is whether the type of program, as measured by the five-point scale of intensity and scope, affects the nature of descriptive representation. Do programs ranking high on the scale attract participants more representative of the neighborhood, less representative of the neighborhood, or is there no measurable difference?

In her review of representation, Hanna Pitkin reminds the reader that central to the theory of many democratic scholars is the notion that democratic government implies an accurate reflection of the community.[35] Often says Pitkin, democratic theorists invoke the analogy of a map or a picture and argue that the representative assembly, in a democratic system, ought to be as representative of the body politic as a map is of the terrain it proposes to depict. One legal theorist is quoted by Pitkin as saying, "Truly, as the map represents meadows, cities, and villages, the legislative body, too, is to form a condensation of the component parts of the people . . . according to their actual relationships."[36] Pitkin notes that proportionalists (as she calls them) have been criticized for neglecting the realm of political action and that some charge that "their zeal for accurate reflection in the composition of the legislature has made them blind to the importance of its governing activities."[37] However, she argues that this is not true since those who have traditionally favored precise representation do so precisely because they expect that the composition of the representative body will determine its activities.

In her essay, Pitkin concludes that the demographic composition of a representative body ought to be only one criteria upon which its representativeness should be judged. She urges, in addition, that substantive representation, which accounts for the representative's influence in his orientation, also be considered. Nevertheless, Pitkin does demonstrate the importance of descriptive representation for much of democratic theory, and it is clear that this issue, including the question of whether or not quota systems should be developed and enforced, is very much relevant to contemporary American politics, as witnessed by the 1972 national political conventions. Indeed, few areas of the OEO and Model Cities programs have been the focus of as much political strife and friction as that concerning the demographic makeup of the various boards and commissions.[38]

Thus concerned with the implications of descriptive representation, a vast number of studies have investigated the characteristics of those who participate in politics for comparison with their constituency. Lester Milbrath, in fact, finds that "the *greatest* quantity of research on political participation has related that behavior to social-position variables."[39] In his study of political activists in the United States, Great Britain, and Russia, for example, Donald Matthews concludes that "political decision-makers are not a cross section of these societies. . . . We have found that they tend to come from near the top of the society's system of social stratification."[40] Other studies which document this same conclusion (that political participation is positively associated with SES variables) include those by Axelrod,[41] Bollens,[42] Bonjean,[43] and Zimmer and Hawley.[44]

Of even more direct relevance to this research are those studies indicating a positive relationship between SES and awareness of and participation in various neighborhood CAA and Model Cities programs. Examining neighborhood awareness of one CAA, Eustace and Carol Theodore found that "the higher the occupation, education, or income category, the greater is the percentage of respondents who know about the CAA," and that "individuals in the upper SES categories indicate greater personal CAA contact than . . . low SES respondents."[45] Likewise, in his study of eight neighborhood OEO boards in Pittsburgh, Gilbert found that the board members, "quite consistently stand above their supposed constituents: they earn more money; they are more likely to own homes; and they are considerably more educated, with almost enough advanced degrees between them to start a small college. It is reasonable to infer from the data . . . that congruent membership is lacking in the Pittsburgh program."[46]

As a final example, in their study of an OEO program in Seattle, Walter Grove and Herbert Costner found that "community residents most easily recruited and most likely to continue as participants [in the local OEO program] seem to be relatively advantaged residents of the area who are already participating in other associations, rather than the 'hard core' poor. Whatever the benefits of participation, the unaffiliated and unintegrated are not likely to be reached, nor are their viewpoints necessarily well represented by their slightly more advantaged neighbors."[47]

In summary, the issue of how accurately a political organization reflects its constituency is important both to democratic theorists and contemporary American politics. In general, it is assumed that those organizations more closely representative of their constituency in a descriptive sense are more likely to accurately reflect the constituents' opinions. As was noted above, Gilbert has argued that constituents will more readily identify with groups possessing social and psychological characteristics which are congruent with their own. Thus he believes that the more congruent programs—those in which demographic characteristics of the representatives most accurately reflect those of the neighborhood—are most likely to succeed.[48] However, a vast amount of survey research, including that dealing with CAA and Model Cities groups, has shown that those active in political organizations tend to disproportionately represent the upper SES categories, relative to their own constituency. The ranking of the twenty-six programs visited for this study allows the examination of whether differing program-types may affect this well-established relationship.

In order to compare the social and demographic characteristics of these program members with those of their neighborhood, it was necessary, of course, to gather background information on each. Such information from each participant was gathered by the questionnaire administered during program visitation. Information on the demographic characteristics of the neighborhood was gathered from census-tract data.[49] In this analysis, three demographic variables are used as measures of descriptive representation. These are: percentage graduating from high school; median income; and median school years completed. For each of the twenty-six groups, a ratio of the members' score on these three items, compared with the neighborhood's score of the same items was constructed. Next, a composite discrepancy ratio score for all groups in each of the five index classifications was calculated (simply averaging the ratios for each program in each category) for each of the three demographic variables.[50] In this manner, three measures of descriptive representation for each of the five program types was developed. This method yields a discrepancy ratio of 1.0 if perfect congruency exists between all those programs assigned a particular index score and their corresponding neighborhoods. Any deviance from 1.0 in a positive direction (i.e., greater than 1.0) indicates that the average score of those participants was higher than their neighborhood; any score less than 1.0 would indicate that the neighborhoods' score on a particular demographic variable was higher than the average for the program members.

As the above discussion of the relevant literature indicates, it is hypothesized that all three ratios will be greater than 1.0—that is, it is expected that the demographic characteristics displayed by the members of these twenty-six programs will be higher than their constituents. Moreover, of particular interest here is the possible effect of the participation index on this relationship. The available literature is silent on this point, however, it is plausible to assume that those programs ranked higher on the participation index will generate more neighborhood interest and involvement and will attract members more representative of the neighborhood (and therefore will have lower discrepancy ratio scores). In any case, the two hypotheses tested in Figure 5-1, are as follows:

Hyp. 5: The demographic characteristics of those participating in all program types will be higher than their neighborhood.

Hyp. 6: The higher the program's score on the participation index, the closer will its discrepancy ratio approximate 1.0 (perfect congruency).

As expected, Figure 5-1 demonstrates that, in every case, the socioeconomic characteristics of those participating in these twenty-six programs are higher than their constituents. This is true regardless of whether one is comparing the percentage of high school graduates, the median annual income, or the median number of school years completed. However, as Figure 5-1 also indicates, the hypothesis that programs ranking higher on the participation index would display discrepancy ratio scores approximating 1.0 is rejected. In fact, a

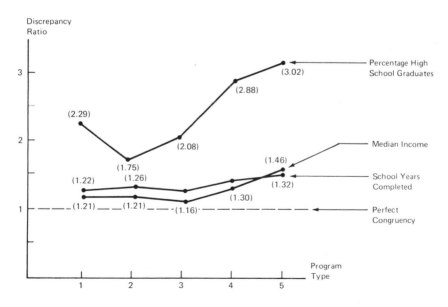

Figure 5-1. Descriptive Representation by Program Type.

relationship almost totally opposite that which was expected is evident. That is, as the program's score on the participation index increases, its discrepancy ratio increases.

Thus those programs ranked higher on the matrix of participation intensity and program coverage apparently attract participants less representative of their constituency than those rated lower on this same index. Based on these findings, one would have to conclude that, if descriptive representation is assumed to be an important element in the evaluation of program success, those rated at the upper ends of the continuum appear less successful than other programs. However, it has yet to be shown that congruent membership is of any consequence for the program's operations and activities. The following section explores the significance of these relationships from this perspective.

Descriptive Representation:
Its Consequences

It was found above that congruent representation was lacking in all these programs and that this discrepancy increased as the program's rating on the participation index increased. The obvious question, then, is: What are the consequences of such representation for the program's operations? In one sense, of course, an answer has already been provided. If one of the objectives of decentralized community activities is to make men more self-governing, then it is apparent (and ironic) that those programs ranked at the higher ends of the participation spectrum are less successful (that is, they engage a less representative section of the neighborhood) than those ranked lower on such an index. This perspective of success is pursued further in the concluding chapter of this study. Here, the question to be examined is more narrowly focused: What is the effect of this discrepancy on the program's operations, organization, and activities? Do programs displaying greater representation discrepancies experience greater levels of internal conflict? Do they spend less time on neighborhood (rather than personal and program) objectives? Is a lesser percentage of the neighborhood aware of these programs? Questions of this nature are also important in the overall process of program evaluation.

As noted above, a number of scholars have argued that congruent (or discongruent) representation may have significant consequences for the operations of a neighborhood program of citizen participation (or, indeed, of any representative body). Perhaps Gilbert is most specific when he concludes that the lack of congruent membership handicaps a neighborhood program in that it becomes difficult to attain cooperation among the members, a sense of membership unity will be lacking and the potential for internal conflict and fragmentation will be high.[51] However, those who make such claims have often been criticized for not empirically demonstrating a link between discongruent representation and program activities and behavior. Over thirty years ago, discussing those studies of demographic characteristics of various legislative bodies, Charles Hyneman warned that "facts about the men who enact statutes are presumably significant only if they bear some relation to legislative behavior—significant only if they affect the content or form of laws, or influence the procedure by which laws are passed."[52] More recently, Pitkin also finds that "we tend to assume that people's characteristics are a guide to the actions they will take, and we are concerned with the characteristics of our legislatures for just this reason. But it is no simple correlation. . . . "[53] Thus Pitkin, Hyneman, and others have argued that an analysis of the demographic characteristics of representatives (and recommendations based on these findings) become truly significant only when one examines the effect of such characteristics on the actions and behavior of the representative body.

The questionnaire administered to participants in the various programs asked a number of questions concerning the internal operations of the programs and the attitudes and awareness of neighborhood residents toward each program. Specifically, the survey asked the respondents to indicate: (1) the extent of internal dissension and conflict in each program; (2) the proportion of time spent on universalistic (rather than particularistic) goals; (3) the program's effect on the neighborhood's general interest in politics; (4) the program's effect on the neighborhood's confidence in local officials; and (5) the proportion of neighborhood residents aware of the program.

Responses to these questions of program operation and neighborhood interest indicated that, although there was a certain amount of agreement among all participants, still a considerable amount of variance was found. Thus about 16 percent reported some degree of internal conflict; about 46 percent reported that less than half of their program time was devoted to matters of neighborhood concerns; almost 60 percent reported fewer than half of all the residents of the neighborhood were aware of the program's existence; and about 23 percent reported that the program had had very little or no effect on the neighborhood's general interest in politics. Again, the primary relationship to be examined here is what effect the representation discrepancy discovered above may have on measures of program operation and neighborhood interest. In order to gauge this effect, simple correlation coefficients between each program's discrepancy ratio and responses to these five questions were calculated. It was noted above that Gilbert argues that when congruent representation is lacking, "it is feasible to assume that the group is neither forceful nor consistent in representing the interests of its constituents," and "the potential for internal conflict and fragementation is high."[54] Others have suggested that programs most accurately reflecting citizen characteristics are more likely to adopt particularistic (rather than universalistic) goals. Alan Altshuler, although he questions the validity of this assumption, portrays the opinions of many who fear that groups of average citizens "have particular handicaps as decision-makers. They have little time to devote to consideration of the issues; their concerns are selfish and immediate. . . . If policies are ever adopted, they tend to be extremely short run. . . . "[55] Indeed, in his three-city study, Paul Peterson found that those programs in which citizen interests were most accurately represented tended to adopt particularistic, short-run goals (such as patronage and personal jobs) rather than universalistic goals.[56] Based on these few surveys, then, it is assumed that neighborhood interest and awareness will be least, internal conflict will be greatest, and the probability of adopting universalistic goals will be highest when representative and neighborhood characteristics are most discongruent. Specifically, the hypotheses to be tested in Table 5-6 are as follows:

Hyp. 7: The greater the discrepancy ratio, the greater the level of internal disagreement and conflict.

Hyp. 8: The greater the discrepancy ratio, the more time spent on neighborhood (universalistic) goals and the less time devoted to individual and program goals.

Hyp. 9: The greater the discrepancy ratio, the less effect the program will have on the neighborhood's general interest in politics.

Hyp. 10: The greater the discrepancy ratio, the less effect the program will have on improving the neighborhood's confidence in local officials.

Hyp. 11: The greater the discrepancy ratio, the less the proportion of neighborhood residents aware of the program.

Those relationships reported in Table 5-6 which are in a direction consistent with the hypotheses being examined are underlined. As that table indicates, all but two of these correlation coefficients are in the proposed direction (and these two fail to meet the 0.05 test of statistical significance). Those relationships which are significant indicate that: (1) an increasing high-school-education discrepancy ratio is associated with greater internal conflict, a worsening of neighborhood trust in local officials, and fewer proportions of neighborhood residents being aware of the program; (2) an increasing median-school-years-completed discrepancy ratio is associated with increasing program conflict and a worsening of neighborhood confidence in local officials; and (3) an increasing income-discrepancy ratio is associated with increasing levels of program conflict. Although only six of these relationships were statistically significant, the general direction of these findings confirms the arguments of those (such as Gilbert) who have suggested that membership congruency may measurably affect a program's operations and the attitudes of neighborhood residents toward that program. To the extent that such a program strives to achieve internal cooperation and harmony, increased neighborhood awareness, and increased confidence in local officials on the part of neighborhood residents, its success may be significantly affected by its representative congruency.

Table 5-6

Effect of Representation Discrepancy on Measures of Internal Conflict, Program Objectives, and Neighborhood Awareness

Questions of Internal Cooperation Objectives, and Awareness	High School Discrepancy Ratio	Median School Years Discrepancy Ratio	Median Income Discrepancy Ratio
1) Extent of internal cooperation and harmony	0.17[b]	0.15[b]	0.14[b]
2) Proportion of time spent on universalistic goals	−0.05[a]	0.09[a]	−0.01[a]
3) Stimulation of neighborhood's interest in politics	0.07[a]	0.08[a]	0.04[a]
4) Effect on residents' confidence of local officials	0.18[b]	0.22[c]	0.01[a]
5) Proportion of neighborhood residents aware of program	−0.23[c]	−0.09[a]	−0.05[a]

[a]Significance Level = Not Significant
[b]Significance Level = 0.01
[c]Significance Level = 0.001

Participant Motives and Descriptive Representativeness: A Summary and Proposed Model

As mentioned throughout this chapter, students of citizen involvement programs have devoted a considerable amount of attention to the motives and demographic characteristics of those participating in these activities. In part, this concern may be attributed to an interest in the effect of such characteristics on the activities and operations of the program, in part this interest reflects a concern with future official acceptance and promotion of citizen participation activities.

This study did not survey the attitudes of local officials toward these programs, however, it seems reasonable to conclude, as have others, that those programs considered by authorities as more of a political and social threat to established norms are less likely to receive funding with the expiration of OEO and Model Cities legislation. It was found, in this sample, that the fear of black desires for racial separation expressed by many is unfounded (surprisingly, a larger portion of white participants favored separate racial and ethnic institutions). However, it was found that, when considering the second and third motives, about a fourth of the participants did seek some form of political mobilization or opposition, and that those individuals were largely found in programs rated at the upper ends of the scope and involvement continuum. Thus, if the assumed official attitude toward citizen participation activities is true, it is to be expected that those programs at the upper ends of the participation scale are less likely to receive future support.

In addition, this chapter is able to make a more definite statement concerning the relationship between the program types, demographic and attitudinal characteristics, and effects on program activities and success. In fact, a model depicting the relationships revealed by this analysis may be schematically presented as in Figure 5-2.

The paths in this model are designated either by a (+), indicating the analysis found at least a moderate relationship to exist or a (0) indicating that only a slight or insignificant relationship was found. As the model indicates, the program type (as measured by the index of scope and intensity) has a significant impact on both the demographic and attitudinal characteristics of those attracted to the various programs. As was noted in the chapter, those programs rated at the high ends of this scale are most likely to attract those whose demographic characteristics are most discongruent with their constituency, and these programs are most likely to attract those whose goal is political-action (rather than social- or welfare-) oriented. It was noted that others have found discrepancies between constituent and representatives characteristics; however, the significance of this model is to suggest that *the greater the program's rating on a scale of program scope and participation intensity, the greater will be this descriptive representation gap. Likewise, the greater the program's score on such an index, the greater the proportion of members likely to be motivated by goals of political action.*

Perhaps the most interesting and significant links are between membership/ constituent congruency, participation motives, and program operations (as rated

Figure 5-2. Proposed Model of Program Typology, Membership Characteristics, and Program Effect.

by the various participants). As discussed above, it has generally been found that a certain degree of discongruency exists between constituency and representatives' demographic characteristics, however, very few have attempted to assess the consequences of such discongruency. The model and the findings presented in this chapter indicate that this discrepancy may indeed have a significant impact on program operations. Especially, it was found that, as demographic discrepancy *increases*, internal conflict tends to *increase*, the program's effect on the residents' confidence *decreases*, and the proportion of neighborhood residents aware of the program *decreases*. To the extent that these concerns are important to the ultimate success of the program, descriptive representation may indeed have a significant impact. Indirectly, of course, this implies that the program type may affect these same concerns since descriptive representation is viewed by the model as a function of program type.

Finally, the model indicates that the link between participant goals and motives and program success (as measured by participant evaluation) is very weak. Although each of the measures used to evaluate this link were in the proposed direction, the magnitude of the relationships was, in each case, found to be slight. This is not to suggest that participant motivations and goals are unimportant. Again, it is suggested that it is this aspect of the program with which local officials may be most interested in their decision to continue supporting such activities. However, in terms of the participants' own evaluations of program success, this link is of only minor importance.

Evidence thus supports the conclusion that variations in program typology can affect participant demographic and attitudinal characteristics. These characteristics, in turn, are important both to the internal operations of the program and to the probability of future support. The implications of this model, as well as other findings reviewed in this chapter, must be somewhat disturbing to those promoting citizen participation as an alternative to the present state of urban politics. It has been found, as reported in numerous studies, that such programs have not yet been able to attract the average neighborhood resident. Rather, those who attend are likely to be relatively better off than their constituents and are likely to already be more involved in a number of organizational activities. In addition, as this study has found, this discrepancy gap is likely to widen as the program scale increases. Those at the upper ends of the scale of scope and involvement are likely to attract members *least* representative of their constituencies. Furthermore, it was found that those programs ranked higher on the participation matrix were more likely to be characterized by internal conflict, a worsening of the neighborhood's trust and confidence in local officials, and fewer proportions of neighborhood residents aware of the program. If, as argued in Chapter 1, a major objective of those participatory democratic theorists promoting citizen participation involves the educational and psychological benefits which supposedly accrue to the average citizen from such programs, it is apparent that the performance of these organizations would be judged as less than successful. Based on available information, it seems fair to conclude that neighborhood participation attracts only the elite of a neighborhood and that this gap widens as the programs approach neighborhood control over broader areas of policy decisions.

However, a final evaluation of neighborhood participation as an alternative strategy to contemporary urban politics is reserved until the final chapter. It is still possible that these programs will be judged by the participants very successful in terms of accomplishing specific goals and will be found to have a positive impact on the participants' trust and confidence in local officials. The following chapter explores these aspects of neighborhood participation.

6

Neighborhood Involvement, Participant Satisfaction, and Citizen Trust

Ira Katznelson and others were quoted in Chapter 1 as finding that citizen participation actually masks two totally different policy objectives.[1] On the one hand, a neighborhood (or citizen) perspective was identified which stresses, above all, a more favorable allocation of goods and services. Also an administrative (or official) perspective was discussed which seeks increased citizen trust and confidence, thus reducing the probability of urban violence. That wide array of studies promoting one or both of these perspectives was presented in Chapter 1, and it is unnecessary to repeat that review here. However, it is important to stress one of the key aspects of all these arguments; that is, the authors present little empirical evidence to support their claims. Thus, as demonstrated throughout this report, the available literature provides a rich supply of hypotheses and assumptions concerning the probable causes and effects of neighborhood involvement but almost no data by which these claims may be assessed. Although this lack of empirical data is true of all phases of the citizen participation literature, it is especially noticeable concerning the proposed consequences of citizen involvement. In this respect, Henry Schmandt is worth citing once again. In his review of the literature he found that "a substantial portion [of the citizen participation literature] is normative in nature. Little is known about what types and degrees of urban decentralization will work and under what circumstances. As yet little evidence is available in the way of systematic analysis or evaluation."[2] This chapter, then, seeks to provide evidence which will allow at least an initial evaluation of the impact of the various policies of citizen participation.

The expectation on the part of citizens' groups that neighborhood involvement will result in improved delivery of goods and services is a straightforward assumption requiring little elaboration. Douglas Yates was quoted above as finding that one of the primary justifications or arguments favoring citizen participation is the belief on the part of neighborhood residents that it "will increase administrative attentiveness and responsiveness to neighborhood needs."[3] Also Joseph Zimmerman finds that those citizens advocating some form of citizen involvement program "argue that large units of government do not necessarily fare better, achieve a higher level of service and more economics, or tax more equitably than small units. Political realities necessitate a new organizational accommodation ... to meet the needs of neighborhoods by ensuring that policies are determined with neighborhood inputs."[4] Applying principles of economic analysis to metropolitan government, Robert Bish concludes that, contrary to what has traditionally been expected, urban services can be more efficiently and equitably distributed by politically decentralized systems.[5] His analysis is too complex to be adequately summarized here, however, Bish persuasively argues that both "political externality" and "social interaction" costs can be reduced by the delegation of decision-making powers and that supply and demand conditions are most effectively satisfied in smaller, homogeneous, units of population. He concludes that "the most efficient use of economic resources takes place when individual demands can be exactly accommodated, as in a purely private-good market. When it is necessary to combine individual demands for a public good, the most efficient political unit for articulating the demand is a relatively homogeneous one. . . . Apparently, individuals with similar tastes for public goods live in the same neighborhoods."[6] As a final example, Alan Altshuler, summarizing the black perspective on citizen participation, believes that minority groups feel that hierarchical structures of local government have been responsible for the formulation of neighborhood programs and policies which differ significantly from the desires of those living in the neighborhood. Those minority groups believe, he says, that "fewer highways and slum clearance projects [as designed and administered by central-ized political processes] are exactly what the cities need. They have inconven-ienced the poor to benefit the affluent. The whole purpose of the participation movement is to redirect public policy so that at least such outrages are impossible."[7] Thus, from this perspective, current centralized and hierarchical methods of urban decision-making are lacking in responsiveness and efficiency and citizen participation will, it is argued, correct these deficiencies to a significant degree.

The theoretical assumptions underlying the second major objective of citizen participation considered in this study—that stressing improved citizen trust and confidence in public officials—are somewhat more complex. One element in this thesis is the argument by many that political behavior is a function, in part at least, of political trust and confidence. Joel Aberbach and Jack Walker suggest that leaders in a representative democracy cannot be successful unless they have gained the trust of the citizenry. They state that "if distrustful groups are denied access to decision-making, or if institutions are too rigid to change, destructive conflict and a breakdown of the social order are possible."[8] Exploring this same theme, Lynne Iglitzin also finds that system confidence "engenders peaceful and willing support of that system. But when that confidence changes to apathy, mistrust, and cynicism, little is required to convert those attitudes into uncontrolled behavior."[9] In his recent essay, Robert Dahl argues that citizen trust favors polyarchy (democracy) while distrust favors "hegenomy" (despot-ism) for at least three reasons. In the first place, trust increases mutual communication which Dahl finds essential for a democratic regime. Secondly, trust permits organizations through which citizens can promote their goals. Finally, conflicts are more threatening, and thus democracy is imperiled, among people who distrust one another.[10]

These scholars, then, all support the thesis that political trust affects political behavior. However, probably the most elaborate (and widely cited) attempt to construct a theory integrating the various elements of this trust model has been provided by William Gamson.[11] One of Gamson's basic arguments is that the tactic which a partisan (citizen) will most likely select in his attempts to influence the political system is a function of his political trust. Conceiving of trust as a continuum (upon which he locates three major groupings—confidents, neutrals, and the alienated), Gamson posits that those at the more confident end of the spectrum will most likely sympathize with traditional and conventional means of political expression such as voting and other nonviolent tactics, and that those at the more alienated extremes will most likely adopt less conventional and more disruptive tactics (mass demonstrations, violence, etc.). Most important, Gamson argues that his is a dynamic rather than static model of influence and discontent. That is, a person's (or group's) ranking on Gamson's confidence continuum is seen as alterable. Just as confident groups can become alienated from the political system, alienated groups can be moved toward confidence. The crucial factor in this exchange, argues Gamson, is the action of government. "A confident group can be moved toward neutrality or alienation by heavy [governmental] reliance on sanctions and insulation. A neutral group can be made more confident by involving its members in relationships that increase identification with authorities.... An alienated group can be made more confident by involving it in a system of exchange with authorities and a series of relationships which encourage identification and internalization."[12]

Thus each of these scholars suggest that political behavior is a function of political trust and that the political-trust orientation can be altered by increasing the channels of citizen involvement and participation in public affairs. These relations can be summarized in the following simplified model shown in Figure 6-1.[13] Aberbach and Walker have documented the proposed relationship between political trust and political behavior (linkage B → C). Indeed, they found in their study that distrustful whites are more likely to favor extremist political candidates and that distrustful blacks are more likely to sympathize with rioters. Thus they conclude "distrust of the government creates a tension in the polity which can build for some time, but ultimately seeks release. Among other things, people can revolt, engage in limited displays of violence like riots, demonstrations, or support candidates for public elective office who give voice to their fears and frustrations."[14]

Figure 6-1. Proposed Model of Participation Opportunities, Political Trust, and Political Behavior.

Studies such as these, then, have provided empirical evidence to substantiate the proposed link between political trust and political behavior.[15] Of primary concern to this study is the proposed link between opportunities for citizen participation and the political-trust continuum (linkage $A \rightarrow B$). As Chapter 1 indicated, an abundance of literature exists which suggests that one means available to authorities seeking to increase public confidence and trust is to increase the channels of direct citizen participation in the process of decision-making. Gamson, himself, was quoted above as showing that an alienated group can be moved to confidence by involving it in a system of exchange with authorities. Likewise, Peter Eisinger has recently argued that one logical hypothesis concerning the relationship between political structure and behavior is that "protest occurs most frequently in unresponsive political systems—in other words, in cities where the opportunity structure is relatively closed."[16]

However, despite this proposed link and in spite of those assumptions outlined above and in Chapter 1, there is almost no empirical evidence to suggest that a program of citizen participation will affect a person's political trust (and ultimately his political behavior) in the supposed manner. Eisinger did find a relationship between form of city government (ranked on a continuum of most open to most closed) and urban protest; however, his study was not concerned specifically with the effect of *neighborhood* programs of citizen involvement. In his study of neighborhood participation programs in twelve cities, George Washnis did conclude that "citizens in all our cities have experienced a new communication link with government which has improved their image of city officials."[17] However, Washnis provides absolutely no empirical evidence to support his claim which appears to be based solely on his own subjective judgment. The single study which has attempted to empirically confirm this link is Louis Zurcher's study of a single OEO program in Topeka, Kansas. Although he did report an improvement in the trust orientation of those participating in this program, the degree of change failed to meet the test of statistical significance.[18]

Thus the justification of citizen participation as a means to increase political trust and thereby alter political behavior has almost no empirical foundation. Although it is generally assumed that some change will occur, there simply is very little data upon which such an assumption can be tested. The purpose of this chapter, then, is to provide the data upon which these two perspectives of citizen participation may be evaluated. On the one hand, the chapter attempts to determine if citizens perceive their participation as effective in improving the delivery of goods and services to the neighborhood; on the other hand, an evaluation of the effect of participation on the citizens' trust and confidence of public authority is attempted. In both cases, the primary independent (causal) variable to be examined is the index of participation previously described. Specifically, this chapter addresses the following four questions: Do neighborhood programs achieve a more favorable delivery of goods and services (as perceived by neighborhood participants)? Does such participation affect an individual's trust and confidence in public authority? What effect does the participation matrix have on these relationships? Can an optimum program be identified which maximizes both goals (delivery of services and improvement of government image)? The following section examines the participants' evaluation of the success of the programs in achieving a more favorable allocation of municipal goods and services to the neighborhood.

Citizen Participation and Improved Delivery of Goods and Services

It was mentioned in the previous chapter that each respondent was presented with several opportunities to express his satisfaction with the program's ability to achieve a more satisfactory distribution of goods and services. In the first place, he was simply asked to rate "the *overall* success of the program in achieving greater benefits and improved services from city hall than otherwise could have been expected." Secondly, each respondent was asked to list three most important projects with which his association had been involved and to rate the "success of the program in achieving satisfactory results in each project." These three project ratings were combined for each individual to form a single index of *project* satisfaction. The effect of the program index on these two measures of citizen evaluation of success is explored in this section.

The few studies which have addressed the question of the effect of citizen involvement on service delivery generally are quite favorable. Although he carefully points out the possible shortcomings and setbacks of programs encouraging neighborhood involvement, John Strange found in his review of the OEO literature that "there are numerous examples available of housing projects altering their leasing and inspection policies, street repairs being made, stop lights being installed, garbage collection and street cleaning activities being increased, highways rerouted, and other alterations in service which are claimed to be the results of the emphasis on citizen participation."[19] Likewise, Washnis (although, again, he provides no evidence to support his claim) finds that in his twelve-city review "the whole process of decentralization has made key officials as well as many employees under them more cognizant of neighborhood problems and more willing to do something about them; therefore the level of department and agency performance has increased"[20] Also, Neil Gilbert, although he admits that the more ambitious goal of "democratization of social welfare was not achieved by the Pittsburgh CAA, concludes that the program "did provide a beginning for many needed services to the poor; Legal Aid, Upward Bound, Head Start, and Day Care were a few of the more excellent services offered through the antipoverty program."[21] Having conducted a survey of members of an OEO program in Knox County, Kentucky, Willis Sutton found that when considering the program impact on such items as educational opportunities, health services, levels of income, and job opportunities, more than 75 percent of those interviewed believed the Community Action program had improved each area.[22] Summarizing much of this literature, Peter Rossi concluded that although "the evidence is only beginning to come in, it does support the claims of the advocates of community organization [that participation can affect meaningful improvement in service delivery]."[23]

Thus it should be expected that those participating in the programs examined for this study generally will report moderate to high levels of satisfaction. It is expected also that the greater the association's rating on the index of participation intensity and program scope, the more successful will neighborhood participants find it to be. Although it appears that no one has empirically examined this last assumption, its validity clearly is implied in much of the literature. Almost by definition it would appear that those at the higher ends of the program index would be more capable of satisfactorily accomplishing a variety of goals. In his discussion of the range of program types, Douglas Yates, for example, describes those programs at the higher ends of the spectrum as those "giving localities control over policy, program, and fiscal resources" which involves "real stakes and *capacities.*"[24] Also, in her essay, Sherry Arnstein argues that those programs at the lowest end of the ladder of participation do not have the "real power needed to affect the outcomes of the political process," and can only "maintain the status quo."[25] Thus the two hypotheses tested in Figure 6-2, below, are:

Hyp. 1: Citizens will generally be satisfied with the program's ability to achieve more favorable allocation of goods and services from city hall.
Hyp. 2: Those participating in programs rating high on the program index will be most satisfied in the program's performance.

As indicated by Figure 6-2, most of those respondents rated their overall program and specific project attempts as successful. On a scale of from 1 to 5 (most to least successful), the mean score of program success was found to be just slightly over 2.0 (or somewhat successful). However, the most interesting relationship revealed in Figure 6-2 is the curvilinear nature of the responses to these items. In contrast to the hypothesis, those ranked at the lowest *and* highest ends of the program continuum found their programs to be the *least* successful. Likewise, those programs assigned the more moderate rankings (2, 3, or 4) were judged by their citizen participants as being *most* successful.

It is possible, of course, that this apparent relationship may be caused more by differences within each program rather than between the program types. That is, it is possible that unmeasured influences—such as those attributable to such characteristics as race, age, education, and so forth—rather than the differing program types, actually may account for the observed variance. However, an

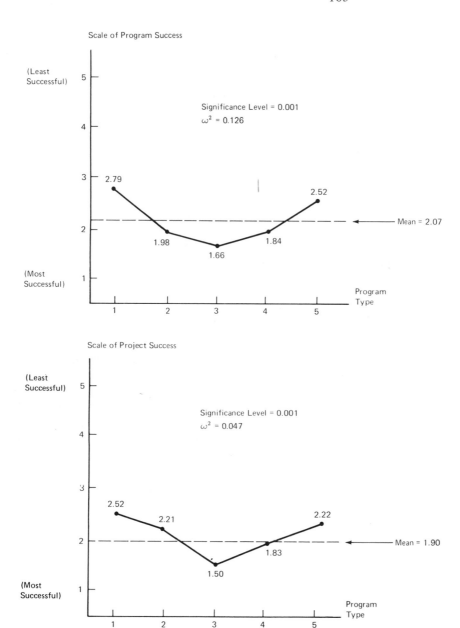

Note: ω^2 (omega squared) is a statistic designed to measure the mount of variance "explained" by the analysis of variance procedure. For a more complete discussion of the interpretation and use of this statistic see: William Hays and Robert Winkler, *Statistics: Probability, Influence, and Decision,* vol. 2 (New York: Holt, Rinehart and Winston, 1970), p. 132.

Figure 6-2. Program and Project Success by Program Type.

analysis of variance test was applied to each set of data and, as Figure 6-2 indicates, this test did indicate that the difference between the program types, after accounting for within program differences, was in each case significant at the 0.001 level. Furthermore, the ω^2 value indicates that the program continuum explains over 12 percent of the variance in overall program satisfaction and almost 5 percent of the variance in the project satisfaction measure. Although it is obvious that other factors are also responsible for the participants' evaluation of the success of each program, it is clear also that the nature of the program itself measurably affects that evaluation. Thus it can be concluded that citizen participants appear generally satisfied with programs of neighborhood involvement and that a program structure can be identified—one which avoids either extreme of the participation matrix—which citizens find most successful. It should be of particular interest to compare the compatibility of this finding with the effect of the program typology on thecitizen's trust and confidence attitudes. The next section explores these concerns.

Citizen Participation and Partisan Trust and Confidence

It has been documented throughout this study that one of the primary motives of many scholars and public officials advocating more channels of direct involvement in public affairs is the anticipation that such participation will improve the citizen's image of government, thus reducing the probability of his selecting violent or disruptive political tactics. Among those numerous reports suggesting a link between lack of participation opportunities, alienation, and political extremism is the influential *Kerner Commission Report* issued immediately following the urban disorders of the late 1960s. Although that report acknowledges the problems of civil disorder to be "imbedded in a massive tangle of issues and circumstances,"[26] one of the primary causes of such disorder was found by its authors to be the lack of sufficient opportunities for disadvantaged groups to express their grievances. They stated that "people in poverty everywhere . . . lack the channels of communication, influence and appeal that traditionally have been available to ethnic minorities within the city and which enabled them . . . to scale the wall of the . . . ghettos. The frustrations of powerlessness have led some to the confiction that there is no effective alternative to violence as a means of expression."[27] Accordingly, the commission recommended the "opening of the channels of communication between government and neighborhood residents. We believe that meaningful community participation and a substantial measure of involvement in program development is an essential strategy for city government."[28]

It has been found, as mentioned above, that the link between alienation and political violence alluded to in the *Kerner Commission Report* appears to exist.

The question to be pursued in this section is the relationship between decentralization and alienation. Does participation in a neighborhood program such as those visited for this study measurably affect one's trust and confidence in public officials? Although it clearly is assumed by many (such as Dahl, Gamson, the Kerner Report, and others quoted in this and previous chapters) that this link is strong and positive, there are those who question this assumption. Aberbach and Walker, although they demonstrated a strong link between alienation and sympathy with disruptive political behavior, express reservations concerning the impact of participation and decentralization on political trust. Considering the various proposals to bolster political trust, they state "there are several policies now being proposed which might [build political trust]. One such option, which has recently received considerable publicity is the decentralization of [city services] into smaller units based on established racial and ethnic communities. Decentralization of the administration of city services along racial lines may be initially satisfying to certain militant elements in the black community, and to many hostile, segregationist whites. We believe, however, that there are serious dangers in any policy which grants legal recognition to the racial divisions within our society and employs them as official administrative categories."[29] Given the importance which the model advocated by Dahl, the Kerner Commission, and others has had for urban public policy, it is crucial that the link between participation and alienation be examined.

In order to estimate the magnitude of the link between participation and political trust, and the effect of the program typology on that trust, three sets of questions are evaluated in this section. In the first instance the participant himself was asked to evaluate the degree to which the participation program had affected both his and the neighborhood's confidence in public officials. Secondly, the participants' response to this question is analyzed by program type in order to estimate the effect of the program index on these responses. Finally, the participants' response to the trust questions developed by the Survey Research Center of the University of Michigan[30] is compared with the expected norm. Answers to these three sets of questions should allow the determination of whether participation affects trust attitudes, the effect of the various program typologies on these attitudes, and the controlled comparison of the participants' trust scores with nonparticipants' trust scores. Together, answers to these questions should provide a reasonably accurate assessment of the strength of the path between citizen participation and political trust. The first question asked the respondent to rate on a five-point scale (from considerably improved to considerably worsened) the program's effect on his and his neighborhood's confidence in city officials to do what is right for the community. The hypothesis to be tested in Table 6-1 is:

Hyp. 3: The respondent will report an increase in both his and the neighborhood's trust in local officials.

Table 6-1

Effect of Program on Participant's and Neighborhood's Trust of Public Authority

	Program's Effect on Trust				
	Considerably Improved	Somewhat Improved	No Effect	Somewhat Worsened	Considerably Worsened
Of Participant	18.3%	46.2%	17.7%	11.3%	6.5%
Of Neighborhood	17.8	48.2	21.1	9.3	3.6

As Table 6-1 indicates, most of the respondents believed that the program had improved both theirs and the neighborhood's image of government.[31] Thus, by their own evaluations, those participants in these twenty-six community programs reported an increase in their trust and confidence attitudes *attributable to* the participation program. The significance of this finding for the trust model is exceedingly important since, as mentioned above, the expectation by many that this link should exist is almost totally unsupported by empirical data.

Having established a link between participation and the participant's evaluation of its impact on his trust attitudes, the second question concerns the effect of the program index on the participant's and his neighborhood's trust attitudes. To what extent are these improved trust scores a function of the type of program which has been established? In the absence of any prior research in this area, it is assumed—as it was when considering the effect of program typology on citizen satisfaction—that the impact of participation on citizen trust will be greater in those programs rated high on the index of participation intensity and program scope. The hypotheses to be tested in Figure 6-3 are:

Hyp. 4: The greater the program's score on the participation index, the greater its effect on the participant's trust attitude.

Hyp. 5: The greater the program's score on the participation index, the greater will be the reported effect on the neighborhood's trust attitudes.

As was the case when considering the effect of the program typology on the citizen's perception of program success, a curvilinear relationship is noted between the program typology and the effect of participation on the improvement of the citizen's trust index. Those programs assigned more moderate scores (2, 3, or 4) are rated by the participants as the most effective in improving both the citizens' and the neighborhoods' image of and confidence in public authority.

As was discussed when considering the effect of the program typology on participant satisfaction, it might be assumed that variations within each program

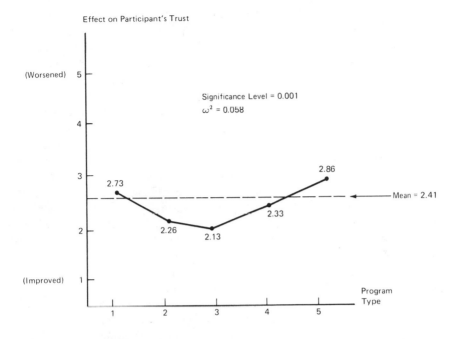

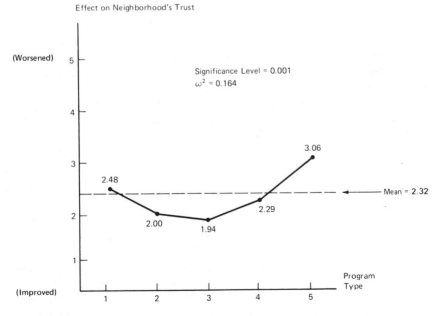

Figure 6-3. Program Effect on Participant and Neighborhood Trust.

type will be found to account for this apparent relationship. Again, however, an analysis of variance test indicated that the effect of the program index on both the participants' and reported neighborhoods' trust in local officials was significant (0.001 level) and that the index accounts for almost 6 percent and over 16 percent, respectively, of the variance in each attitude. It is obvious here, too, that other variables affect the participants' and neighborhoods' improved confidence in local officials but that the program index has a measurable impact.

The data presented so far, then, indicate that participation may have a positive effect on partisan trust and confidence attitudes and that the nature of the program may significantly affect that relationship. However, the material presented to this point has not incorporated a control measure so that it is impossible to compare the attitudes of participants and nonparticipants. The thesis presented above, that participation measurably affects political trust, would be greatly strengthened if it were shown that those who have been associated with a program of neighborhood involvement display trust and confidence scores higher than that which would be expected of nonparticipants.

As has been previously mentioned, in order to gather this information each respondent was asked to complete the trust questions administered by the SRC. In this manner participants' responses may be compared with the expected norm (as established in the latest SRC survey). Whatever differences are found, then, may be inferred as caused by participation. Although this method of inference obviously lacks the rigor of a sophisticated before-and-after experimental design, it is an accepted tactic of social science research. In his review of the strategies available to the social scientist, Herbert Hyman labels the technique utilized here as a form of "Semisecondary Analysis."[32] The essence of this approach, as explained by Hyman, is the argument that norms established by surveys of groups unexposed to the treatment being investigated can be compared with responses of those exposed to the treatment (in this case, participation) and the observed differences may be attributed to the activity under investigation. In the absence of such established norms, as Hyman suggests, the researcher is free to "indulge in fictitious comparison imputing a different pattern to a comparison group he has not measured, simply on the basis of his beliefs."[33] However, the comparisons available from previous surveys considerably improve the investigator's confidence that whatever differences are observed are due to the treatment effect and not the researcher's preconceived beliefs. Hyman goes on to argue that comparisons of this sort are most meaningful when the researcher uses the exact questions as used in the control survey and when the researcher is able to break down his respondents into refined norms so that the effects of extraneous variables (such as race, region, city size) are effectively controlled.[34]

This method, then, is applied to the available data in an attempt to more accurately estimate the effect of participation upon citizen trust and confidence in public officials. In order that these comparisons are most meaningful, only those respondents in the SRC survey from the midwestern states who reside in cities of a size comparable to those visited for this study were examined. The first figure to be presented below examines the effect of the participation index on: (1) the respondents' overall trust score, as measured by an index comprised of all the SRC trust questions; and (2) the respondents' ranking on the direct trust question, "How much of the time do you think you can trust the government to do what is right—just about always, most of the time, some of the time, or never?" Based upon the findings presented above, the hypothesis to be tested in Figure 6-4 is:

Hyp. 6: Regardless of program type, the participants' trust score will be higher than the expected (control) norm as established by the SRC survey.

As Figure 6-4 indicates, it is found that in almost every instance the participants' score on both the trust index and the single, direct trust question are higher than the expected norm. Also, the curvilinear relationship noted in the previously examined charts is maintained. Thus the evidence continues to support the proposition that participation will measurably affect the citizen's trust in public authorities.

It remains, then, to be determined if the difference between the participants trust score and the expected norm is a significant difference. Table 6-2 compares the mean scores of each group's (participants and nonparticipants) response to the direct trust question: "How much of the time do you think you can trust the government to do what is right?" In order to make this test most meaningful, blacks and whites are compared separately.[35]

The results presented in Table 6-2 indicate that the difference between the participants' and nonparticipants' trust attitudes is a significant difference.[36] Although the final trust score of participating whites indicated a higher degree of confidence in public officials than that reported by blacks, it appears that the total effect of participation actually is greater on black feelings of trust and confidence than whites, as indicated by the larger mean difference of black scores (it should be mentioned that, as coded, the higher the score the greater the *distrust*). In either case, the improvement in the respondents' reported image of government was found to be statistically significant (0.001 level), thus further supporting the crucial linkage between neighborhood involvement and political trust.

Although the combined weight of the evidence presented in this section does support the possibility of a causal link between participation and trust, it does not, of course, preclude the possibility that those who participate do so because their trust is initially higher. Thus it might be argued that the more trusting are more likely to participate and that the true sequence of causality is exactly opposite that inferred above. It is true that survey research has documented an apparent correlation between trust and participation. However, it has been found that, when controlling for other variables, there is no reason to assume

112

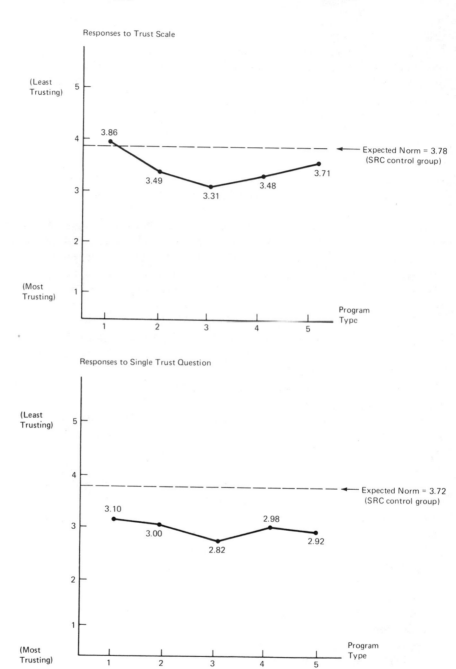

Figure 6-4. Trust Scores by Program Type Compared with Expected (Control) Norm.

Table 6-2
Mean Trust Scores[a]

Group	Blacks	Whites
Control (SRC) scores	4.47 (N = 60)	3.52 (N = 222)
Treatment (participant) scores	3.21 (N = 82)	2.87 (N = 299)
Difference =	1.26	.65
t = 7.41	t = 5.91	
Significance = 0.001	Significance = 0.001	

[a]Mean responses to the single, direct trust question, "How much of the time do you think you can trust the government to do what is right?" are used in the construction of this table. When examining the mean differences of the responses to the entire trust scale, the results are similar except that the t scores are not quite so large.

that the more trusting are more likely to participate in political activities. William Erbe's study is of particular interest. Using "higher order partialling techniques," he concluded that his findings "raised grave doubt as to whether alienation affects political participation independently of socio-economic status. . . ."[37] In sum, the present study has found significant differences between the trust attitudes of those participating in neighborhood organizations and control groups reflecting the expected trust scores. Since previous survey research has questioned the independent effect of trust attitudes on participation, it is reasonable to conclude that the differences in trust scores reported above are due, in part at least, to the act of participation.

This section, then, has indicated that both in a subjective sense (when the respondent is asked to evaluate the effect of participation) and in an objective manner (when the participant's trust score is compared with the expected norm) participation appears to improve the respondent's image of the political system. This is true both of black and white participants. Again, the importance of this finding is that it lends empirical support to a model, promoted by many social scientists, which suggests that increasing channels of communication and participation will improve levels of political trust and increase confidence in public authorities. In addition, the findings support a variety of policy-related conclusions discussed in the concluding chapter.

The significance of these findings become even more apparent when considering the combined results of the impact of program typology on both citizen satisfaction and improved confidence as illustrated in Figure 6-5. As indicated in Figure 6-5, an optimum zone of program typology can be identified which maximizes both values of citizen satisfaction and improved citizen trust. Trust and satisfaction are lowest in those programs rated at the lowest *and* highest ends of the program index. Likewise, trust and satisfaction are reported to be

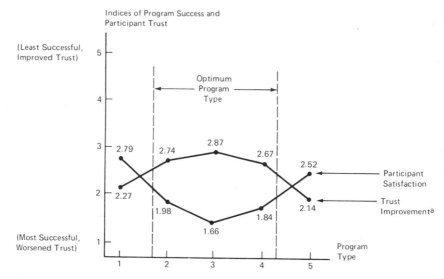

Indices of Program Success and
Participant Trust

aThe trust index has been reversed from its presentation in Figure 12 in order that the "zone of optimum program typology" may be emphasized.

Figure 6-5. Program Success and Effect on Participant Trust by Program Type.

greatest in those programs assigned more moderate values. The significance of these findings to citizen groups and urban officials contemplating the initiation of a program of neighborhood participation are obvious. Regardless of whether success is measured in terms of citizen satisfaction with the program's ability to improve the delivery of goods and services or defined in terms of improved citizen trust and confidence, the most successful programs will be those avoiding either extreme of the intensity and scope index. The concluding section speculates upon some possible reasons for these relationships.

**Conclusion: Citizen Participation,
Citizen Trust, and Program Satisfaction**

As mentioned at the outset, one model of political behavior which guides much social science research posits causal relationships between channels of citizen involvement, citizen trust and confidence, and political tactics. It is generally argued by those supporting this model that increased means of citizen involvement in public affairs will increase the citizen's trust and confidence in public authority, which, in turn, will reduce the likelihood of the citizen's reliance on tactics of violence and disruption in his attempt to influence the political system. It is based upon these sets of assumptions that many public officials in the 1960s and 1970s abandoned their traditional concerns of economy, efficiency, and professionalism in the management of public affairs and advocated, instead, some form of citizen participation. The link between citizen trust and political tactics has been fairly well explored and substantiated by previous research. The less trusting, it has been found, are more likely to sympathize with, and engage in, extremist political tactics. The crucial link of that model, that between participation and trust, has received almost no empirical support. The wide variety of programs visited in this study permitted not only the testing of this link, but also allowed the determination of the effect of the various program types on the trust index. It was found that most participants did report an improved image of the political system and that, when compared with cohorts in a control sample, the improvement among blacks and whites was highly significant.

In addition to this, it was found that an optimum zone of program typology can be identified which maximizes *both* the values of improved trust and citizen satisfaction. Trust and satisfaction are reported least favorably affected at the extremes of the program typology and most positively altered at the more moderate program values. A few possible explanations, and an expanded model, of these relationships, are presented below.

On the one hand, the finding that participants at the lower ends of the program index are least satisfied and report the least improvement in trust is hardly surprising. These programs, it will be recalled, are very narrow in scope receiving little or no assistance from city hall. These programs are representative of those which Sherry Arnstein labels as being "manipulated" by city hall and, as the hypotheses indicated, it was expected that the results would appear as reported.

The surprising aspect of the material presented in this chapter, of course, is the extent to which those participating in programs rated at the higher ends of the spectrum consistently reported results similar to those participating in programs ranked at the lower ends of the spectrum. Initially, one might assume that differences within each program category possibly could account for these results, rather than the program typology itself. However, the analysis of variance tests reported above indicated that the effect of the program index remained significant when accounting for internal variance and that this index, by itself, accounted for a measurable portion of the variance in each dependent variable. While the available data do not permit a conclusive explanation of these findings, several possible contributing factors can be suggested.

At the most basic level, one might consider the application of the rising-levels-of-expectation model, often cited as a possible explanatory thesis of unrest in cross-national comparisons.[38] According to this view, discontent is most likely to occur when disadvantaged groups first begin the process of development.

According to de Tocqueville, "revolutions are not always brought about by a gradual decline from bad to worse. Nations that have endured patiently and almost unconsciously the most overwhelming oppression often burst into rebellion against the yoke the moment it begins to grow lighter."[39] This thesis is cited by the Kerner Commission as one of the contributing causes of the urban violence of the 1960s. In their report, the commission stated, "Negro attitudes [in the 1960s] were changing. In what has been described as a 'revolution in expectations,' Negroes were gaining a new sense of self respect and a new image. . . . Ironically, it was the very success in the legislatures and the courts that, more perhaps than any other single factor, led to intensified Negro expectations and resulting dissatisfactions with the limitations of legal and legislative programs."[40] Applying this thesis to the data presented in this chapter, one might conclude that the level of expectations would be greatest among those participating at the highest ends of the program index and that their inability to achieve dramatic and immediate improvements would result in the observed attitudes of less participant satisfaction and greater levels of distrust. Interestingly, one of the officials interviewed for this study cited this thesis as the cause for discontent among the programs in his city rating highest on the scale of participation intensity and scope. When asked why citizens in these programs displayed greater levels of dissatisfaction and alienation than those in other programs, he stated:

The program [of citizen participation] raised the level of alienation by raising the expectations. When you tell people there is something better they can have and then you can't deliver because the system is so cumbersome, then they become frustrated. You plop down to the neighborhood a grand plan and you say, "here, you have 2.9 million dollars to spend" and they have no idea what you are talking about. . . . They become very frustrated and their only way to react toward city hall is to become belligerent. So as a consequence some of these programs became very belligerent and destructive. . . They destroyed themselves, they destroyed the school system, they destroyed the city.[41]

According to this thesis, then, participants at the upper ends of the program continuum can be expected to display greater levels of hostility toward city hall for a reason similar to that often applied to citizens of modernizing nations. When the expectations of citizens are rapidly raised and gratification is not immediately forthcoming, so the theory would argue, they are likely to become frustrated, angered, and potentially hostile.

A second possible explanation for those groups rated highest on the participation continuum displaying higher levels of program dissatisfaction and less of an improvement in trust attitudes can be derived from Paul Peterson's study of participation programs in Chicago, Philadelphia, and New York. In that survey, Peterson also noted that "the greater the level of influence by community representatives over the program, the greater the level of conflict. . . . As representatives of the poor gained more control over the allocation of poverty program resources, they found more at stake to divide them."[42] Peterson's explanation, then, simply is that as citizen control is increased over a program's resources and directions, the participants will find more cause for internal division, thus raising the general level of frustration and dissatisfaction with the program. In New York's program, which Peterson rated as the one in which citizen control was greatest, he found intense and severe conflict among the citizen groups vying for power. He stated, "During this period [1964-66] the conflict between Negroes and Puerto Ricans in the heterogeneous community of East Harlem [over control of the program's funds] became so intense that on more than one occasion physical force was threatened."[43]

Thus far two possible explanations for participants in programs—rated at the upper ends of the program continuum—displaying increased levels of frustration, internal conflict, dissatisfaction, and alienation have been reviewed. The first suggests that the rapid raising of citizen expectations, and the inability to provide immediate satisfaction, contributes to this syndrome; the second argues that increased control leads to internal divisiveness as differing power groups compete for control. While each of these undoubtedly is of merit, both fail to completely account for the observed relationships. In the first place, applying either theory, one would predict that those groups at the lowest end of the program spectrum (where levels of expectation and struggle for control of resources should be the least) would have the highest score on measures of satisfaction and trust. Of course, this was not the case. The participants' responses to questions of satisfaction and alienation at both ends of the program index were almost identical. Furthermore, both of these theories places the blame for these attitudes almost totally upon the citizen participants, ignoring possible influences of other actors. It seems self-evident that success or failure of a program designed to increase channels of communication between the neighborhoods and city hall should be shared by all involved.

One theory which is relatively consistent with all sets of data presented above has been presented by Michael Lipsky.[44] Lipsky distinguishes between two categories of rewards which authorities may disperse: symbolic and material. Furthermore, he believes, the kind of reward obtained from political action may have a significant impact on the group organized to receive a particular reward. Lipsky states that "if that activity [political organization and protest], once engaged in, is rewarded primarily by the dispensation of symbolic gestures without preceptible changes in material conditions, then rational behavior might lead to expression of apathy and lack of interest in politics or a rejection of conventional political channels as a meaningful arena of activity."[45] It was found, as documented above, that groups at each end of the program continuum found their participation least successful in achieving greater benefits and improved services (material rewards). It should not be surprising then, Lipsky would argue, to find that these groups are found to be least trusting in the political system.

This thesis, although it provides at least a partial account for those at each end of the continuum displaying higher distrust scores, obviously begs the question of why those groups are less successful in achieving material rewards. Assuming trust (distrust) may be a function of program success, as Lipsky's thesis would imply, the remaining question is why are those programs rated high on the program continuum less successful in achieving material rewards than those assigned more moderate values? One explanation for this phenomenon has been offered by James Sundquist and David Davis.

In their study of CAAs and Model Cities programs in eight states (twenty-nine programs), Sundquist and Davis argue that these two programs represent two models of community organization. The first model, represented by CAAs, stresses program independence of city hall, the vigorous challenging of the status quo, innovation, and the raising of a myriad of questions about how America's communities have served the poor. This model, in short, "is adept at defining and sharpening conflicts but unsuited to resolving them, and not suited for community wide coordination."[46] The second model identified by Sundquist and Davis, represented by Model Cities programs, stresses coordination of activities (rather than innovation), planning conducted by citizens *and* public officials, and greater control throughout exercised by city hall.[47] As indicated in Chapter 2, it is apparent that those programs rated at the upper ends of the program continuum developed for this study closely resemble Sundquist and Davis' CAA model, and that those ranked near the midpoint of the scale resemble their Model Cities model. Significantly, Sundquist and Davis also found that satisfaction and morale were consistently lower in the CAA model than in the Model Cities programs. Even when interviewing staff members of the various CAAs, they found that "those closely associated with the program often made comments indicative of frustration and low morale."[48] In addition, these researchers found, as did Peterson, that internal conflict was greater in the CAA model. "The directorship—and to an even greater degree the subordinate staff positions [of CAA programs]—sometimes became the object of patronage scrambles."[49]

They noted two fundamental reasons for the CAA model being found to be less successful than the Model Cities programs. The first was the conflict with other community organizations (including city hall) that arose when the CAAs began to challenge the status quo; the second was the adverse community impressions of the organization. They quote a civic leader in one city visited as saying, "The reason it [the CAA] lacks 'clout' is that the city as a whole does not have confidence in it as a responsible agency."[50] By contrast, they found Model Cities programs to have been much more favorably received by community participants as well as by public authorities. The Model Cities program, they note, involves a considerable amount of coordination and direction from city hall while still maintaining the concept of maximum citizen participation in the planning process. Thus they find the community as a whole is more willing to accept as legitimate (and nonthreatening) the Model Cities model and this acceptance, they feel, is essential to program success. Although such a model obviously sacrifices an emphasis on innovation and confrontation, they argue that it is more likely "to enlist the cooperation efforts of public and private agencies, to provide a structure within which a city's elected officials can exert energetic leadership, to mobilize resident participation in the formation and execution of plans, and to resolve conflict."[51] In sum, the Model Cities approach, they feel, is more likely to succeed because its emphasis on coordination by city hall insures a greater support by the community at large.

Interestingly, Hallman also notes this need for a balance between coordination and participation in neighborhood programs. He states, "on the one hand, coordination emphasizes the centripetal forces of community power. The exercise of those controls comes most easily when they are in the hands of one person or relatively few. This points toward the mayor and other elected officials as the ones who should have responsibility and authority for allocating funds and for assuring that they are used in a manner that achieves coordinated activities. On the other hand, citizen participation is a centrifugal force. As involvement increases, more actors enter the arena, . . . competition for scarce resources comes into play, and various interest groups contest against one another."[52] Hallman goes on to argue that a successful policy for neighborhood participation programs is one which brings into harmony these two forces.

It is suggested here (although this argument obviously requires further empirical testing) that those programs ranked near the midpoint of the continuum constructed for this study do combine the centrifugal-centripetal (participation-coordination) forces identified by Sundquist and Davis and Hallman. The centrifugal forces of those programs, rated lower on the participation continuum developed for this study, certainly will be less threatening (simply because, by definition, citizen factions have less control over scarce resources), and those programs should be less likely to experience the sorts of internal conflict noted by Peterson. Just as important, however, those programs ranked near the midpoints of the continuum will involve a considerable amount of interaction with, and coordination and direction from, city hall. This coordination, Hallman, and Davis and Sundquist argue, is necessary if the community as a whole is to accept as legitimate the program; and this community acceptance, in turn, they believe to be essential to the program's success.

In any case, several possible explanations for the relationships found in this chapter have been offered. The first two emphasize characteristics of the citizen participants of the various programs (lack of expertise, rising expectations, greed, etc.); the others stress the combined factors of official coordination and community support. It is suggested, finally, that these various explanations might be combined to form a single hypothesis. Those participating in programs ranked near the midpoint of a continuum such as that presented above can be expected to report greater levels of improvement in trust attitudes and higher levels of program satisfaction because: (1) internal conflict is reduced (Peterson); and (2) program coordination, direction and legitimization (as defined by public officials and the community at-large) is increased (Sundquist and Davis); thus (3) facilitating the delivery of material, rather than symbolic, rewards (Lipsky). A more formal model of these relationships might be presented as in Figure 6-6. This model simply illustrates the important links suggested by the hypothesis presented above. Program type is seen as affecting the program's legitimacy which affects the program's probability of achieving material rewards which, in turn, affects both the participants' feelings of satisfaction and attitudes of trust. It is stressed that this study has supplied evidence only to support a relationship between program type and participant satisfaction and improved trust. The endogenous variables appearing in Figure 6-6 (legitimacy and material rewards), although supported by the literature reviewed above, are presented as hypotheses only—subject to future documentation.

It is emphasized that the significant findings of this chapter are: citizens will find their program at least moderately successful in accomplishing its goals; participation will increase one's political trust and confidence in public authority; the actual effect of participation on trust attitudes and citizen satisfaction will vary by program type; and an optimum zone of program typlogy can be identified which maximizes both the values of participant satisfaction and citizen trust. As more and more local officials confront the question of whether to support citizen participation programs after the conclusion of the OEO and Model Cities legislation and, if so, what sort of program to adopt, these findings should be of obvious interest. The concluding chapter develops a summary model of the findings reported in this and the preceding chapters.

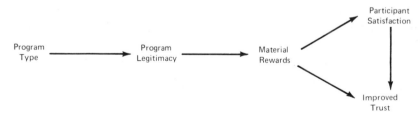

Figure 6-6. Proposed Model of Program Type, Legitimacy, Rewards, Satisfaction, and Trust.

7

Conclusion: Policy and Theoretical Implications

In his excellent treatise on participatory democracy, Daniel Kramer notes ironically that at a time when many Western nations have adopted wide-ranging systems of social services and liberal policies, groups of left-wing persuasion in those countries appear most unsatisfied.[1] This is so, he says, because contemporary radicals "contend that Labor-Britain, 'Gaulist-Pompidouist France,' America's 'Great Society,' all suffer from the same basic flaw: they are centralized bureaucracies which are fundamentally undemocratic in the sense that the ordinary citizen has no voice in determining the policies that emanate from them. . . . "[2] In place of this centralized social welfare state, Kramer asserts, these groups are advocating a system of participatory democracy, one designed to make men more self-governing.[3] This is, of course, essentially the same point made by the more recent democratic theorists cited in Chapter 1 of this study. In various counties this left-wing agitation has resulted in differing policies incorporating principles of participation. In Yugoslavia, West Germany, and Austria, for example, workers have formed worker councils designed to provide the laborer a greater share of management activities.[4] In the United States, this participation movement has focused mainly on inner-city, often low-income neighborhoods. Sponsored by such federal programs as OEO and Model Cities, hundreds of community participation programs throughout the country were established in the late 1960s. These programs have had significant implications for urban policy, political behavior, and metropolitan government; accordingly, a substantial body of literature exists attempting to explain the environmental factors associated with citizen participation and the actual effect of participation for the citizen and the system as a whole.

However, this study began with the premise that the available literature is deficient in several crucial areas. It was found, in the first place, that much of the literature is normative and lacks empirical foundation. Although this literature provides a wealth of hypotheses concerning the expected effects and probable outcomes of citizen participation programs, there is almost no evidence to support the various claims. Secondly, that evidence which is available is largely of the case-study variety. The obvious limitation of the case-study approach is that it provides neither the grounds for constructing valid generalizations or for proving (disproving) established hypotheses.[5] Thirdly, it was argued that most available surveys suffer from an inadequate conceptualization of the participation issue. That is, although recent observers clearly distinguish between several degrees or types of citizen participation programs, the available literature largely ignores these distinctions. Participation, then, has been treated almost exclusively in a nominal fashion (either a city has a participation program or it does not) thus confusing important implications. Finally, it was noted that much of the data collected to date reflects public official or academic evaluations of citizen involvement, largely ignoring citizen input. Since, as demonstrated above, success or failure of such a program is largely dependent on citizen reaction to the program, it is essential that this perspective be incorporated in any study attempting to evaluate programs of citizen involvement.

This study, then, did attempt a policy analysis of citizen participation programs which: (1) collected information from several ongoing programs of neighborhood involvement; (2) utilized a conceptual scheme facilitating meaningful inter- and intra-city comparison; (3) relied heavily upon citizen input. From this analysis, a policy model of the conditions associated with and the effects of programs of citizen participation emerges. Figure 7-1 presents this model.

As this model indicates, the type of citizen participation program adopted by a community is at least partially a function of that community's social and political environment (links $A \rightarrow C$ and $B \rightarrow C$). Also, the type of program adopted was found to have significant implications for the demographic characteristics ($C \rightarrow D$) and motives of citizens ($C \rightarrow E$) attracted to participate. These characteristics, as well as the program typology, were found to measurably affect various activities of the program as well as the citizens' evaluation of program success. Throughout this study an attempt has been made to relate these various findings to the relevant social science literature, and a summary of the most important of these is presented in Table 7-1. It is unnecessary to repeat here those findings presented in Table 7-1 which already have been discussed in detail in the analytical chapters of this report. Instead, this concluding chapter focuses on the major policy and theoretical *implications* of the model presented in Figure 7-1 and uses the data generated by this study, as well as other available information, to come to at least a tentative judgment concerning the viability of

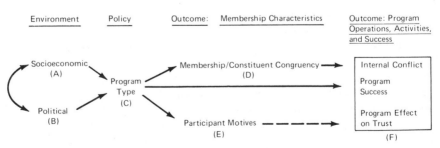

Figure 7-1. Summary Policy Model.

Table 7-1
Summary of Major Hypotheses

Effect Of	Participation Index	Participant Motives	Descriptive Representation	Participants' Evaluation of Success	Participants' Political Trust
			Effect On		
Population	+				
Affluence	0				
Federal support	+				
Reformed political structure	0				
Ethnicity	0				
Race	+				
Mayor's voting power	+				
Urban violence	+				
Participation index		+	+	±	±

Note: A + indicates a positive effect
A ± indicates a curvilinear relationship
A 0 indicates no observed relationship
A blank indicates hypothesis not tested

decentralization as an alternative to the existing state of urban government. This model and the data presented above have significant implications for the study and implementation of urban policy, democratic theory, and future research needs. Each of these is discussed below.

**Implications for the Study and
Implementation of Urban Public Policy**

The implications of this analysis for both the study and implementation of urban public policy are several. Among the most important of these for the study of urban politics include the relevance of a cultural theory of politics to urban America, the impact of federalism on urban policy, and the consequences of policy alterations for adult political socialization.

It will be recalled that a major hypothesis tested in Chapters 3 and 4 was that cultural differences would account for at least a portion of the variance in the participation index. It was argued that citizen involvement represented a particularly appropriate test of the cultural theory as formulated and applied to urban politics since such involvement is almost completely antithetical to those values attributed to one classification of urban culture (that sometimes called "public-regarding ethos"). It was found in those chapters that, even when employing all commonly used measures of urban culture, this variable was of almost no explanatory value. Considered in the context of other studies reporting similar results,[6] it was concluded that the cultural thesis of urban politics, if it can be salvaged, is in need of considerable revision. These findings, it is suggested, have significant implications for the explanation of urban policy in the United States.

On the one hand, these findings suggest that it is the cultural *similarity* of American cities, rather than their *differences*, which is the most profound aspect of cultural relationships in the United States. Although it cannot be argued that cultural differences did not in some earlier period differentiate between the political orientations of various localities, the outstanding feature of contemporary urban America, it would appear, may well be its cultural unity. In their study of federalism, James Sundquist and David Davis make this same point. They state: "The nation for decades has been steadily coalescing into a national society; the advances of communication and transportation, the nationalization of the economy, and the sheer physical congestion of population have destroyed the isolation of . . . communities."[7] William Shaffer found that "although there are very important interstate cultural differences, the American states are more profoundly characterized by their cultural similarity."[8] It is stressed that the present study did not test for patterns of cultural variety among American cities, however, it is apparent that the weight of the evidence supports the suspicion, at least, that cultural differences, if they exist, are minor.

Whatever the significance of a so-called national culture for other areas of American social and economic life, its implications for the study of state and local politics are profound. For years, as noted in Chapters 3 and 4, scholars have employed cultural explanations in their attempts to account for state and urban policy differences. Now, it would seem from the evidence which is available that there simply is very little cultural differentiation among American communities; and thus, of course, such a measure cannot account for the variances in American subnational politics. This does not mean that differences in policy orientations of American states and communities do not exist; obviously they do. It does mean that variables other than those purporting to measure cultural differences will have to be articulated, measured, and examined.

One such variable which this study has demonstrated is of considerable importance in explaining the policy variations in American cities is federal policy. Unquestionably, the receipt of federal funds designated for the promotion of programs of neighborhood and citizen participation dominated this study's attempt to explain a city's response to the citizen participation movement. This finding dramatically illustrates the results of the changing nature of American federalism which Sundquist and Davis have labeled the transformation from a pattern of "shared" responsibilities to a pattern of

"Washington-initiated and Washington-led" programs.[9] Under the older pattern of shared responsibility, federal assistance, they argue, was initiated as a "means of helping local governments accomplish *their* objectives." In the newer model, "the federal grant is conceived as a means of enabling the federal government to achieve *its* objectives."[10] Although it is undoubtedly true that no area of urban policy-making has been more affected by the influence of this changing nature of American federalism than the communities' response to citizen participation, it is apparent that other areas of community decision-making have been similarly influenced. In fact, argues Michael Reagan, the great "bulk of public services in the area of health, education, welfare, housing, highway construction, police protection, parks and recreation, conservation practices, and agricultural extension" today is conducted by state and local governments, with financial assistance and policy direction from Washington.[11] This study, then, has demonstrated the tremendous influence which federal practices may have for urban policy.

It would be of particular interest to discover how those relationships presented in Chapters 3 and 4 may be altered with the demise of OEO and Model Cities legislation and their replacement with programs of General and Special Revenue Sharing. Reagan, especially, distinguishes between the potential effects of categorical and block grants. Categorical grants (examples of which he includes OEO and Model Cities legislation) "are by and large those for specifically and narrowly defined purposes, leaving little discretionary room on the part of a recipient government as to how it uses this grant. . . . " On the other hand, block grants (such as Revenue Sharing) "are broader in scope and although tied to a clearly stated area, . . . they do not specify the exact objectives of permitted expenditure and hence create much larger zones of discretion on the part of the receiving government."[12] It would be expected, then, that with the passage of Revenue Sharing, urban policy decisions in all affected areas will be less influenced by federal direction and more affected by variations in local environment, leadership traits, and public opinion. At the very least, this study has demonstrated the overwhelming influence of federal policies in the 1960s and early 1970s on the urban policy of citizen participation, and it is therefore suggested that the relative importance of other influences (perhaps even some version of the cultural theory) may be found to be largely a function of changing patterns of federalism.

These findings have even broader implications for the study of urban policy and particularly to the extent that they suggest linkages between policy decisions and patterns of adult socialization. As suggested in Chapter 5, political scientists have long been concerned with the impact of differing structural arrangements on political attitudes and behavior. It was also noted in that chapter that differing structural arrangements have been found to affect such behavior as race riots, voting behavior, and protest behavior.[13] This study, and others cited above, found significant alterations in citizen attitudes and opinions attributable to participation in programs of neighborhood involvement.

The implications of these findings are of obvious significance for the study of urban politics. It would suggest that the manner in which citizens acquire their political beliefs and attitudes are functions not only of the childhood socialization processes and of the resources they may marshal but also, in part at least, of their adult political experiences. The suggestion that adult experiences may be important in the socialization process is hardly startling.[14] However, the vast majority of socialization research has focused only on early childhood experiences as they relate to later political behavior.[15] The findings presented here would suggest that important changes in political orientation may occur well into the adult years of an individual's life and that alterations in policy output (especially when considering programs involving citizen-government interaction and involvement) may significantly affect that process. At least, as Dale Marshall argues, findings such as these would suggest that programs of participation "ought not to be looked at solely as mechanisms for efficient job performance" but also as agents of socialization. They serve as arenas in which political attitudes are being shaped, loyalties and self-images are being influenced."[16] Viewed as possible agents of political socialization, a number of interesting questions—not generally considered when assessing the results of citizen participation programs—may be asked. In addition to being concerned with the material rewards of participation, one might also consider as important indicators of a program's success its effect on: the participants' knowledge and understanding of politics; personal confidence and political skills; tolerance of the views of others; participation in other activities; and so forth.

In a more general sense, it appears that important political attitudes of the adult population are, to some degree, alterable and that policy variations, as they affect an individual's contact with the political process, may significantly influence these attitudes. It is suggested that policy scientists consider more carefully the socialization effects of public policy when examining and evaluating outcomes and impacts of public policy, especially those policies designed to promote increased citizen-government contacts.

Of course, the findings of this study have direct policy implications for the implementation of future programs of citizen involvement. A principle theme running throughout this study is that, although a variety of citizen participation programs have been adopted, little empirical evidence is available by which the effectiveness of the several types may be evaluated. In addition, it is argued that with the phasing out of the OEO and Model Cities programs and the passage of Revenue Sharing measures, city administrators will again be confronted with the decision of what type, if any, program of citizen participation should be developed. Thus it seems that the results of this study could be of immediate significance for those urban officials and neighborhood groups contemplating the future direction of citizen participation programs.

It was found, as reported above, that programs encouraging citizen influence may measurably affect the citizens' trust and confidence in local officials. The effect of participation on the trust variable was measured in several ways. In the first place, the participant, was simply asked whether or not participation had improved his confidence in local officials "to do what is right for the community." Almost 70 percent of those included in this study indicated that such participation had improved their trust in public authority. Recall data of this nature obviously must be interpreted with caution, but at least it indicates that people believe their participation has positively influenced their trust. When objectively comparing the trust attitudes of these participants with a control group, a significant improvement in the trust attitudes of black and white respondents was found. Thus the evidence strongly indicates that participation can significantly improve the citizen's confidence in public officials. Since, as discussed in Chapter 1, such an improvement is a major policy objective of public officials advocating programs of citizen involvement, it seems likely that these results would be interpreted by local officials as favoring the continued support of these programs.

Furthermore, it was found that citizens, for the most part, rated their programs as successful in achieving greater benefits and improved services from city hall for their community. From both perspectives, then, citizen participation was judged by those interviewed for this study as successful.

However, the most important policy consideration emerging from this study involves the specification of the program type which most effectively accomplishes both goals. As discussed in Chapter 6, an "optimum zone of program typology" was identified which maximizes both objectives. The programs comprising this zone were those avoiding either extreme of the program typology. The programs near the midpoints of the continuum, it was hypothesized, are viewed by the community as more legitimate; therefore, their probability of achieving material rewards is increased, and the evaluation of the program's success by neighborhood participants and its effect on their image of local government is enhanced.

It is thus suggested that the most successful programs will be those of a compromise nature. That is, those programs in which control by neighborhood residents is sacrificed for a degree of direction and coordination by city hall will be judged the most effective. Peter Marris and Martin Rein have suggested that the goals of coordination by city hall and the representation of neighborhood interests are in conflict and that some compromise should be sought. They conclude that "the Federal Government should be prepared to support, in the same community, both official and counterveiling conceptions of a viable programme."[17] This study lends empirical support to those scholars such as Marris and Rein (and others reviewed in Chapter 6 such as Sundquist and Davis and Hallman) who argue that programs designed so as to encourage maximum input *both* from citizens and city hall, but which maintain ultimate responsibility for direction and control with city officials, will be the most successful. It would be concluded, then, that future implementation of citizen participation programs should devote at least as much attention to the *types* of program initiated as to other factors previously considered important (such as the proportionate makeup of the segments of the community represented).

Implications for Democratic Theory

As mentioned in the introductory chapter, a number of democratic theorists today are challenging what has been labeled as the "contemporary" theory of democracy. That theory, it has been argued, is not focused on the participation of the average man in political affairs. Rather, in the contemporary model of democracy "it is the participation of the minority elite that is crucial and the non-participation of the apathetic, ordinary man lacking in the feeling of political efficacy, that is regarded as the main bulwark against instability."[18] In place of this model, participatory democrats would advocate programs encouraging the direct involvement of the average man in the decision-making process. These more recent theorists, it was suggested in Chapter 1, are less concerned with the stability of the system and are more interested in the psychological and educational benefits which would supposedly accrue to the body politic from participation. Primarily on this point, the role of the average man in the affairs of the state, those supporting the contemporary model of democracy and those supporting the participatory model are in obvious, and seemingly irreconcilable, conflict. Does democracy require only the competition among elites for whom the electorate periodically casts its vote, or does democracy require the active participation (or at least the opportunity to participate) of all its citizens in all aspects of the political process?

The data provided by this study cannot, of course, prove either one of these models to be correct. What is attempted here, using both the data generated by this study and other available information, is the construction of at least a crude operational definition of the participation model of democracy and the determination of whether the available evidence supports the linkages between participation and the consequences predicted by such a definition. At the very least, such an exercise should assist in the determination of whether programs of neighborhood participation such as those visited for this study are successful in achieving the goals of the participatory model. Should the data indicate that these programs are not successful in accomplishing these objectives, this would not, of course, indicate that the objectives are to be abandoned but it would indicate the need for advocates of participatory democracy to seek additional means for their accomplishment.

Again, the participatory democrats are concerned with the psychological benefits of participation. Among those qualities which Carole Pateman suggests the theorists of participation believe to result from direct democracy are "the belief that one can be self-governing, confidence in one's ability to participate responsibly and effectively, and [the confidence] to control one's life and environment."[19] To a considerable extent, these traits are similar to those defined by political scientists as traits of political efficacy. *Political efficacy* has been defined as "the feeling that political and social change is possible, and that the individual citizen can play a part in bringing about this change."[20] Likewise, it has been suggested that the politically efficacious citizens are those who believe "the affairs of government can be understood and influenced by individual citizens."[21] It seems, then, that the concept of political efficacy is quite similar to the psychological and educational benefits which supposedly accrue from participation. In fact, Pateman argues that "the sense of political efficacy or competence [may be taken] to be an operational definition of, at any rate part of, the psychological effect referred to by the theorists of participatory democracy."[22] And yet it seems that another dimension of participation is important in the development of an operational definition. This dimension would account for the number and variety of citizens affected by a program of participatory democracy. One of the most "cherished goals of the supporters" of participatory democracy, argues Kramer, is "the creation of a citizen body the *majority* of whose members are self-governing."[23] Those programs appealing only to the community's elite would be rated less successful on this dimension than one attracting the sustained participation of a substantial cross-section of the community. It is suggested here, then, that a program designed to achieve a more "self-governing citizenry" can be judged to be successful to the extent to which it: (1) positively affects the political efficacy and confidence of those involved; and (2) enlists and maintains the active involvement of the average citizen. From the perspective of the theorists of participatory democracy, these would seem to be the most basic requirements of a successful program of citizen involvement. Again, the purpose of this section is to evaluate the success of programs of neighborhood participation in accomplishing these goals.

As to the first requirement, the development of feelings of political efficacy, both the evidence from this study and from other available sources indicate that programs of neighborhood involvement are at least moderately successful. The standard efficacy scale developed and administered by the Survey Research Center of the University of Michigan[24] was administered to those participating in these twenty-six programs, and their scores were found to be higher than the expected norm (again, using as a control the same method described in Chapter 6). However, this alone is an inadequate method of evaluation. It has long been known that the more efficacious are more likely to become involved in political movements in the first place.[25] However, the conclusion that participation may improve efficacy is buttressed by other surveys using more rigorous experimental methods. In her study of a single OEO program in Los Angeles, Marshall concluded that "there were indications of increases in feelings of efficacy [among the neighborhood participants].... The increases in the community representatives' feelings of effectiveness and in their information may be linked with increased participation. . . ."[26] Reviewing the vast amount of literature concerned with participation in work-related activities, Pateman concluded that "the major [efficacy] arguments of the theory of participatory democracy on the politically important psychological impact of participation . . . have been shown to have considerable empirical support."[27]

These observations were reinforced by the personal visitations of those programs included in this study. In every case, it was apparent that the program had increased the amount of community information available to the participants and had improved their skills in dealing with city hall. The author was continually impressed with the amount of preparation and research conducted by the organizations prior to discussions of community matters and at least a third of those programs attended had scheduled for the same evening presentations by officials of city hall on various aspects of municipal government. Typical topics for discussion included such immediate, if somewhat mundane, matters as proposed increases in bus rates, trash pick-up and removal, city housing codes, the coming fiscal budget, proposed tax increases, city welfare services, and so forth. Only 8.8 percent of the participants surveyed indicated that officials of the local government never attended their meetings for the purpose of presentations and discussions. In other instances, the groups discussed various tactics and methods by which their influence could be strengthened. Three of the programs had invited presentations by candidates for city council positions in order that they might decide whom their organization should support in the coming municipal election. One group had recently purchased a mimeograph machine so that leaflets could be distributed throughout the neighborhood. Another group devoted a portion of a meeting to drafting a letter of protest to be sent to their city commissioner concerning cutbacks in program financing. The overall impression gained from program visitations was that these groups have become quite knowledgeable of their community's political affairs and were very much aware of their own potentials, and limitations, as political organizations. This impression was echoed by interviews with members of city hall. One staff person commented, "If someone [governmental agency] tries to maneuver around them, they now know how to maneuver right back."[28] When asked to list the major accomplishments of the programs in his city, another official stated, "The major accomplishment is the [improved] sophistication of the groups—the fact that they can come up to city hall and get things done. When they first started, they couldn't find their way around. Now anyone of them could take my job—they taught themselves."[29] Still another city official said, "they [the community groups] know their way around my office better than my own staff."[30]

Based on the available evidence, it seems appropriate to conclude that participation in programs of neighborhood involvement can improve the educational and psychological traits (efficacy) of citizens, thus satisfying the first requirement established above. However, the record is much less encouraging concerning the degree to which programs of neighborhood participation have been able to promote widespread community involvement. Although all meetings visited for this study were open to all residents of the neighborhood, it was found in almost every case that the elected members of the program's board or council far outnumbered the neighborhood attendants. In almost a fourth of the meetings, in fact, no neighborhood residents other than elected representatives were present.[31] This lack of concern on the part of the neighborhood is supported by a vast number of studies of neighborhood voting patterns. In the selection of initial board meetings for OEO programs, typical turnout rates were: Watts—1 percent; Boston—2.4 percent; Cleveland—4.4 percent; Kansas City—5.0 percent; Philadelphia—3.7 percent; New York City—10.0 percent; Staten Island—5.5 percent; Manhattan—9.0 percent; and so forth.[32] Discussing the problems of organizing neighborhood residents in Philadelphia, Sherry Arnstein (writing for the neighborhood participants) notes that "the community people are daily struggling with basic bread-and-butter survival issues for themselves and their families. Attempts to organize them around their mutual problems for their mutual gain are doomed unless they can see tangible results of their efforts."[33] Reflecting on statistics such as these, Kramer comments, "It is highly unlikely that the average inhabitant of these areas [those in which programs of neighborhood involvement exist] even tries to convince his representative on these boards to implement a particular project he thinks would help the community; the extremely low turnout in the election to fill the positions [on the boards] is ample evidence for this."[34]

Perhaps just as disappointing was the finding of this study, reported in Chapter 5, that those programs potentially most capable of achieving the goal of a self-governing citizenry (those rated high on the participation scale) are likely to be the least representative of the neighborhood. Those programs affording greater citizen influence, control, and independence appear to attract the elite of the neighborhood, discouraging participation by the average citizen.

Thus it seems reasonable to conclude that programs of neighborhood involvement may satisfy one of the requirements of participatory democracy but have yet to demonstrate its ability to satisfy the other. At best, it seems that the decentralization of municipal political and administrative functions will provide only *some* people greater exposure to decision-making and will present opportunities for the training in the art of self-government of which only a few will take advantage. As Kramer concludes, decentralization "will make a few people more self-governing as individuals than at present; will teach a few who would not otherwise have learned how to govern wisely and well. [But] it is not likely to achieve . . . the creation of a citizen body the majority of which are self-governing."[35]

To repeat, this analysis has not provided evidence which would prove the superiority of one theory of democracy over the other. It has shown that programs of neighborhood government, which have been advocated by many participatory democrats, are likely to only partially satisfy the minimum requirements of a participatory society. Neither does this mean that the objectives of participatory democrats are without merit; just that other means for accomplishing those objectives should be sought. This is not the place to consider, in depth, other areas to which the principles of participation may be extended; however, it might be appropriate to indicate at least one alternative.

An area of particular interest is at the level of job-related opportunities. As indicated at the beginning of this chapter, work councils (through which employees share a degree of management in industry) have been established in several European countries. Indeed, Peter Bachrach, a widely cited participatory theorist, specifically argues that it is in industry-related positions that programs of participation are most likely to succeed. He states, "For many individuals political issues and elections appear either trivial or remote; . . . of a different magnitude are issues which directly affect them in their place of work, issues which are comparatively trivial, yet are overlaid with tensions and emotions that often infuriate and try men's souls. Political education is most effective on a level which challenges the individual. . . . "[36] In her review of participation opportunities in European industry, Pateman concludes that the empirical evidence available "gives us no good reason to suppose that the democratisation of industrial authority structure is impossible, difficult and complicated though it may be."[37] It appears possible, then, that programs designed to provide the worker a more direct means of participation in industrial decision-making may prove more successful at accomplishing both criteria established above. It would at least extend the opportunity of participation to greater numbers of individuals. In any case, if the benefits of participation are to be valued, it would seem that the application of the principle of direct involvement to spheres of activity other than neighborhood politics should be sought. Work-related opportunities provide one such option.[38]

Future Research Needs

Prior to formulating a judgment as to the viability of the strategy of citizen participation, this brief section offers a few suggestions concerning future research priorities. Some of these suggestions are empirical in nature, some are of more theoretical importance. Many of these have been introduced above, however, it is appropriate to review these needs collectively in the hopes that future research might benefit from these observations.

It is often suggested, at the conclusion of social science research, that additional studies of the topic under investigation are necessary prior to a final evaluation. However valid this observation may be of other areas of social science research, it seems particularly applicable to the study of neighborhood organizations. Together, some 2500 rural and urban communities have received funds either from Urban Renewal, OEO, or Model Cities since their inceptions.[39] There are also hundreds of neighborhood programs receiving funds from various sources such as United Fund, the Ford Foundation, the National Federation of Settlements and Neighborhood Centers, and various church-affiliated institutions.[40] In addition to these, of course, there are thousands of neighborhood groups, relying solely on membership dues or contributions for support. While the author is well aware that some larger city programs, near universities, have been saturated with students and faculty seeking information,[41] it is also true that only a fraction of this total has been systematically examined. This void is especially apparent when considering programs involving either rural *or* upper SES communities.[42] It would be particularly interesting to compare the motives and results of programs involving these various socio-economic and demographic groupings. In addition to needing more studies of differing varieties of programs, studies employing more rigorous and conclusive methods of social science research are required. Apparently the only study of neighborhood participation employing techniques of random sampling was that conducted by Brandeis University, and that study was concerned only with OEO programs existing in larger metropolitan areas.[43] Also the application of before-and-after research designs are needed before an accurate estimate of the effects of participation can be judged. The problems involved in constructing and applying such rigorous designs are obvious, but the interest in, and importance of, the topic of neighborhood decentralization would seem to warrant such an effort. In addition, there are a number of very basic questions, rarely considered, which should be of interest to the urban scholar. To what extent is program success based on specific leadership qualities? What effect do attitudes of city officials have on the program's success? Are programs consisting of racially and ethnically mixed individuals more or less successful than the more homogeneous programs? We have, at present, almost no information concerning questions such as these.

As a second level, it has already been mentioned that future research would benefit by broadening the definition of success and failure of programs of neighborhood involvement. It became apparent to this researcher, as it has to others conducting field examinations of such groups, that these neighborhood programs serve more than just the accomplishment of specific job and task needs. These programs, in fact, appear to be important agents of adult socialization and could be profitably examined from that perspective.

Thirdly, it seems apparent that studies of the effects of other measures designed to extend the objectives of direct participation and involvement in decision-making should be sought. This study and others have shown that participation in neighborhood organizations, although it may positively affect citizen efficacy, has been able to attract the sustained involvement of only a very small proportion of the community. If the goals and objectives of those labeled here as "participatory democratic theorists" are to be valued, it seems obvious that other means by which they may be accomplished should be explored. The opportunity to participate in job-related experiences was briefly examined above. Other options include university, church, and even family-related spheres of activity.[44] Here, it is only suggested that we have almost no empirical evidence concerning the effectiveness of participation in these other areas and that such evidence is needed in the overall evaluation of the participation strategy.

Finally, and in a more theoretical vein, the whole question of the desirability of decentralization certainly should not be considered a closed (i.e., universally accepted) issue. Even assuming the possibility of optimum conditions—those in which a maximum number of people are able to receive the psychological and educational benefits of participation—one might still question the value of such a strategy. Some of the most important disadvantages of decentralization are discussed below and will not be introduced here. It is only mentioned that additional social and political options have been suggested and that decentralization is not the only alternative to the present structure. Kramer, for example, promotes a system which he labels "centralized socialism"—one in which the central government would own and manage the major units of the economy, but in which a preference would be shown for "small factories and small stores controlled by consumers and neighborhood councils." Such a system, he says, would be a better device than either the present system, or any form of decentralization, in insuring "the provision of a decent standard of living for all, the efficient use of scarce resources, and the lessening of racial tension."[45]

The purpose of this section is not to defend decentralization against proposals for centralized socialization. The following section does attempt a tentative evaluation of decentralization as an alternative to the present state of urban politics, but it should be clear from this discussion that additional research is required before a final judgment is possible and that alternatives even to policies of decentralization are worthy of theoretical and philosophical exploration.

Conclusion and Evaluation

It seems appropriate, in conclusion, to draw on the data presented in this study to formulate at least a tentative judgment concerning the desirability of decentralization as an alternative to the present state of urban politics. It has been found that programs of neighborhood involvement are likely to: (1) increase the participants' confidence and trust in local officials; (2) achieve, at least in the participants' own judgment, a more favorable allocation of goods and services (material rewards); and, (3) improve the participants' political efficacy, competency, and skills. Obviously these are impressive accomplishments, however, a major disadvantage of these programs, as noted above, is their ability to attract the involvement of only a very small portion of the neighborhood. Prior to a final evaluation, it is necessary to at least briefly consider other possible side-effects of neighborhood participation.

In the first place, it is not clear, even in optimum conditions, whether the balance of the benefits of citizen participation do in fact flow in the direction of the neighborhood. Particularly troublesome is the concept of political trust, examined in some detail in this study. Evidence was presented to support the conclusion that participation may increase political trust; yet, as was emphasized throughout, this clearly is a goal supported by authorities, not neighborhood residents. Trust may even be viewed as dangerous if it serves only to encourage apathy or unquestioned obedience on the part of the citizen. As David Easton defines the term, "political trust is a kind of diffuse support which forms a reservoir of favorable attitudes or good will that helps members to accept or tolerate outputs to which they are opposed or the effect of which they see as damaging to their wants."[46] Likewise, William Gamson argues that trust may become a "problem for partisan leaders" when it is converted into apathy on the part of the citizen.[47] Thus it is clear that increasing the level of political trust is potentially dysfunctional from the perspective of the neighborhood organization or partisan leaders. Actually, this problem, as it relates to neighborhood participation programs, may be less serious than it would at first appear. It was found in Chapter 6 that trust was associated not only with the act of participation but also with the citizen's perception of program success. Thus it was those programs best able to accomplish material rewards in which trust was most positively affected. As long as the increased level of trust is accompanied by the improved delivery of service, as was the case here, the exchange seems just.

Of even more concern to some is the possibility that programs of neighborhood organization may be used (co-opted) by urban officials to bolster their sources of political power. James Wilson was quoted in Chapter 4 as finding that "many new style mayors are trying to build up neighborhood associations and enter into relationships with old ones in order to provide themselves with a way of reaching the average voter and of commanding his support."[48] Ira Katznelson is bitterly opposed to practices of this sort. He states, "For rulers [city officials], decentralization holds out the possibility of recreating buffering linkages between citizens and the polity, linkages which the rulers [city officials] can use to integrate the polity more successfully." Furthermore, Katznelson argues, "when one looks at decentralization programs through these lenses, the ambiguities recede, and the essential comes into focus. The basic issues is one of legitimacy and control. Decentralization [may become] an instrument of the mimetic urban counterrevolution that seeks not to raise but to mask structural issues of power."[49] The evidence gathered in this study indicates that city hall does expect political support from neighborhood programs. When one official was asked if the mayor expected the voting support of those organizations in his city, he commented, "I would hope to God that if we [city hall] do something for someone they remember us. You hope that someone you help would say 'thanks a lot' and the best way they can thank a politician is to vote for him the next time he comes up for support."[50] In addition, over 53 percent of those participating in the programs visited for this study agreed with the statement that "city officials sometimes expect the electoral support of your Association in return for their support of your Organization's projects." Thus it appears that city officials do, at least to some extent, expect the electoral support of neighborhood organizations and that neighborhood participants, themselves, agree with this observation. To the extent that these two concerns (an emphasis only on increased trust and mayorality strength) are real, the potential for co-option and manipulation exists and must be considered in a final evaluation of citizen participation programs.

Others are concerned not so much with the problem of program co-option as with the ultimate effects of such participation on social relationships. The argument sometimes presented is that today's most important social problems will only be exacerbated by programs of neighborhood involvement. It was mentioned in Chapter 5 that many have expressed a concern with a potential racial separationist attitude of those favoring neighborhood organizations. However, it was found in this study that the vast majority participating in these programs favor racial integration, not separation. Nevertheless, the problem persists than an emphasis on community and neighborhood development neglects contacts between neighborhoods. According to Kramer, "if one surveys the conflicts that threaten the world most today, quarrels among neighbors will not be found. The most ominous antagonisms, at least on an intra-national level, involve clashes between racial and religious groups. The hatred between white and black in the United States is only the most obvious example."[51] The emphasis on neighborhood participation, he believes, "reduces the already-too-sparse personal contacts between those residents and the inhabitants of another area populated by a different group. This in its stead would lessen the chance that the tension between the two groups could be amicably resolved."[52] Kramer concludes that the "sort of community which decentralization is most likely to further, the tie between like and like, may threaten the growth of bonds between unlike—the links the world needs most today."[53] Decentralization of municipal services and administration from this perspective, regardless of its short-range benefits, is likely in the long run to have little significant impact on the most important social relationships of contemporary America.

Perhaps most damaging of all, in the evaluation of decentralization as a viable strategy, is the charge that it not only may increase the friction between racial and ethnic groups, but that it cannot be truly effective in solving urban America's most pressing problems. The essence of this argument is that the major problems facing America's cities cannot be solved at the neighborhood level. Kenneth Clark, although generally sympathetic with the decentralization movement, concludes that such a tactic "must function in light of the probability that deprivation in many areas, such as education and employment, may not be responsive to programs of . . . community action. The problems of poverty cannot be resolved as if they were isolated from the wider economic, social and political patterns of the nation."[54] Also according to Henry Schmandt, "the forces that maintain deprivation and alienation—among them institutional racism, low income, unavailability of jobs, and under-employment— are largely beyond the pale of neighborhood action."[55]

These are some of the major disadvantages of decentralization which have to be considered. It is argued that decentralization may only be a method of co-opting and manipulating neighborhood groups, that it may neglect and even discourage urgently needed contacts between racial and ethnic groups, and that it really cannot solve the most pressing problems of urban America.

Citizen participation, then, has both advantages and disadvantages. Clearly, it will not solve all the problems facing America's cities nor will it, by itself, accomplish a self-governing citizenry desired by participatory democratic theorists. However, it does appear capable of solving a few problems and of providing a few people with opportunities to participate in politics which they would otherwise not experience.

The final judgment, as to whether the net benefits of participation outweigh the possible disadvantages, obviously depends on one's priorities. This study, and especially this final chapter, has attempted to present an impartial accounting of both sides of the debate. From the perspective of this author, the merits of neighborhood participation—at least on the limited scale practiced in most American cities—far outnumber its potential demerits. It has been shown that citizen participation can improve the delivery of goods and services to the neighborhood, can improve political trust, and can make at least some people more self-governing. Those who expect that neighborhood involvement can accomplish more than this, or that it is free of limitations, probably will continue to be disappointed; and yet, as mentioned above, these are impressive accomplishments.

The message of this study, in conclusion, seems to be that it would be unwise either to completely desert those programs of neighborhood involvement already established or to place total confidence in citizen participation as a means of ameliorating the urban crisis. The most rational federal policy toward citizen participation appears to be one which provides considerable discretion to individual communities in determining whether to adopt a program of citizen involvement, and the most rational policy for individual urban areas is one promoting programs avoiding the more extreme forms of neighborhood control and large-scale decentralization efforts. If the implications of Revenue Sharing for citizen participation as discussed in this study (especially Chapter 4) are correct, this is precisely the policy most likely to emerge in the immediate future.

Notes

Notes

Chapter 1
Introduction: Citizen Participation,
Democratic Theory, and a Method of
Classification

1. Peter K. Eisinger, "Community Control and Liberal Dilemmas," *Publius* 2 (Fall 1972), pp. 129-48.

2. Carl W. Stenberg, *The New Grass Roots Government?* (Washington, D.C.: Advisory Commission on Intergovernmental Relations, 1972), p. 3.

3. Joseph F. Zimmerman, *The Federated City* (New York: St. Martin's Press, 1972), pp. 11-21.

4. Daniel P. Moynihan, *Maximum Feasible Misunderstanding* (New York: The Free Press, 1970), p. 8.

5. Maurice R. Stein, *The Eclipse of Community* (Princeton: Princeton University Press, 1960), p. 280.

6. As quoted in Moynihan, *Maximum Feasible Misunderstanding*, p. 10.

7. See: William Kornhauser, *The Politics of Mass Society* (Glencoe, Illinois: The Free Press, 1959).

8. Moynihan, *Maximum Feasible Misunderstanding*, p. 11.

9. Kornhauser, *The Politics of Mass Society* esp. p. 77.

10. Stein, *The Eclipse of Community*, pp. 284, 296, 329 (emphasis mine).

11. Moynihan, *Maximum Feasible Misunderstanding*, p. 12.

12. Peter Bachrach, *The Theories of Democratic Elitism* (Boston: Little, Brown and Company, 1967), p. 101.

13. Jack L. Walker, "A Critique of the Elitist Theory of Democracy," *The American Political Science Review* 60 (1966), pp. 285-95.

14. I am referring here to democratic theory as formulated by Dahl, Berelson, Satori, and others after the Second World War. This theory is discussed in the sections which follow.

15. Carole Pateman, *Participation and Democratic Theory* (Cambridge: Cambridge University Press, 1970), p. 1.

16. Bernard Berelson, Paul F. Lazarsfeld, and William N. McPhee, *Voting* (Chicago: University of Chicago Press, 1954), p. 307.

17. Ibid., p. 312 (emphasis in original).

18. See Bachrach's critique of this perspective in: Bachrach, *The Theories of Democratic Elitism*, pp. 33-35.

19. Pateman, *Participation and Democratic Theory*, p. 7.

20. For an excellent critique of Schumpeter's theory see: Geriant Parry, *Political Elites* (New York: Praeger, 1969), pp. 144-47.

21. Joseph A. Schumpeter, *Capitalism, Socialism and Democracy* (New York: Harper and Row, 1956), p. 269.

22. See: Robert A. Dahl, *A Preface to Democratic Theory* (Chicago: University of Chicago Press, 1956); Giovanni Sartori, *Democratic Theory* (Detroit: Wayne State Press, 1962); Raymond Aron, "Social Structure and the Ruling Class," *British Journal of Sociology* 1 (1950), pp. 1-16.

Although the views of Dahl, Sartori, and Aron are similar, there are, of course, important differences. In his study of New Haven, Dahl describes the political system as a form of "polyarchy." Such a system contains a large number of political resources which are unequally distributed among its members. Equal participation, then, does not exist in the polyarchy, nor does a single elite. Rather, groups of minorities and their leaders will tend to be specialists in their own issue areas. Out of this clash of competing interests, argues Dahl, policy will emerge which is most likely to approximate a consensus of all concerned. Sartori views democracy as a procedure in which leaders compete at elections for authority. The key to the survival of democracy, in Sartori's opinion, rests in the hands of the ruling elite. For Sartori, democracy is dependent on the quality of its leaders. Also for Aron, the degree of autonomy possessed by the elites of a society is a measure of the health of democracy. Aron insists upon the plurality of elites as a prerequisite for democracy, but clearly views democracy as a static process—one which does not require the political emergence of deprived groups.

23. This argument is best presented in Dahl, *A Preface to Democratic Theory*, Appendix E.

24. Bachrach, *The Theories of Democratic Elitism*, p. 5.

25. Pateman, *Participation and Democratic Theory*, p. 24 (emphasis mine).

26. Peter Eisinger, "Protest Behavior and the Integration of Urban Political Systems," *The Journal of Politics* 33 (November 1971), p. 981.

27. Pateman, *Participation and Democratic Theory*, p. 31.

28. Walker, "A Critique of the Elitist Theory of Democracy," p. 293 (emphasis in original).

29. Pateman, *Participation and Democratic Theory*, p. 42.

30. Ibid., p. 43.

31. Moynihan, *Maximum Feasible Misunderstanding*, p. 179 (emphasis in original).

32. The arguments among the contemporary and radical political scientists were reviewed above. For criticisms of the sociological view presented here see: Arthur C. Neal and Melvin Seeman, "Organizations and Powerlessness: A Test of the Mediation Hypothesis," *American Sociological Review* 24 (April 1964), pp. 216-26; Daniel Bell, *The End of Ideology* (Glencoe, Illinois: The Free Press, 1960); and Joseph Gusfield, "Mass Society and Extremist Politics," *American Sociological Review* 27 (February 1962), pp. 19-30.

33. See: Douglas Yates, "Neighborhood Government," *Policy Sciences*, 2 (July 1972), pp. 209-219; and Robert A. Aleshire, "Planning and Citizen Participation," *Urban Affairs Quarterly* 5 (1969-1970), pp. 370-93 for a complete discussion of these justifications.

34. Ira Katznelson, "Antagonistic Ambiguity: Notes of Reformism and Decentralization," *Politics and Society* 2 (Spring 1972), pp. 329-30.

35. For an elaboration of these reforms see: Edward Banfield and James Q. Wilson, *City Politics* (New York: Random House, 1963), and especially their chapter, "Reform."

36. U.S. Advisory Commission on Intergovernmental Relations, *Fiscal Balance in the American Federal System* (Washington, D.C.: U.S. Government Printing Office, 1967), vol. 2, pp. 16-17.

37. National Commission on Urban Problems, *Building the American City* (Washington, D.C.: U.S. Government Printing Office, 1968), p. 350.

38. U.S. National Advisory Commission on Civil Disorders, *Report of the National Advisory Commission on Civil Disorders* (Washington, D.C.: U.S. Government Printing Office, 1968), p. 16.

39. Peter Eisinger, "Protest Behavior and the Integration of Urban Political Systems," *The Journal of Politics* 33 (November 1971), p. 981.

40. Wendy Goepel Brooks, "Health Care and Poor People," in *Citizen Participation: Effecting Community Change*, Edgar S. Cahn and Barry A. Passett, eds. (New York: Praeger, 1971), p. 139.

41. Sumati N. Dubey, "Community Action Programs and Citizen Participation: Issues and Confusions," *Social Work* 15 (1970), pp. 76-84.

42. James Q. Wilson, "Planning and Politics: Citizen Participation in Urban Renewal," in *Urban Renewal: People, Politics and Planning*, Jewel Bellush and Murray Hausknecht (New York: Doubleday, 1967), p. 299.

43. *Bulletin No. 71-3*, Advisory Commission on Intergovernmental Relations, December, 1971, p. 1.

44. David K. Hart, "Theories of Government Related to Decentralization and Citizen Participation," *Public Administration Review* 32 (October 1972), p. 613.

45. Joseph F. Zimmerman, "Neighborhoods and Citizen Involvement," *Public Administration Review* 32 (May/June 1972), p. 207. Reprinted from the *Public Administration Review*, journal of the American Society for Public Administration.

46. It should be noted that what is being labeled in this passage as the "administrative view" of decentralization and which seeks to enhance the legitimacy of the political system also is shared by many urban scholars. Alan Altshuler, for example, states that "the central issues of citizen participation and decentralization are social peace and political legitimacy, not abstract justice or efficiency." Also, Dorothy Buckton James declares one of the major assets of citizen participation to be its potential for overcoming "the alienation, apathy, and despair that has been so destructive." See: Alan A. Altshuler, *Community Control* (New York: Pegasus, 1970), p. 195; and Dorothy Buckton James, "The Limits of Liberal Reform," *Politics and Society* 2 (Spring 1972), p. 317.

47. Reported in: Zimmerman, *The Federated City*, p. 14.

48. Henry J. Schmandt, "Municipal Decentralization: An Overview," *Public Administration Review* 32 (Special issue, October 1972), p. 577. Reprinted from

the *Public Administration Review*, journal of the American Society for Public Administration.

49. Ralph M. Kramer, *Participation of the Poor* (Englewood Cliffs: Prentice-Hall, 1969), p. 5.

50. Wilson, "Planning and Politics," p. 299.

51. Yates, "Neighborhood Government," p. 213.

52. George J. Washnis, *Neighborhood Facilities and Municipal Decentralization* (Washington, D.C.: Center for Governmental Studies, 1971), p. 63.

53. Eisinger, "Community Control and Liberal Dilemmas," pp. 130 and 134.

54. Yates, "Neighborhood Government," p. 213.

55. Quoted in Sar Levitan, *The Great Society's Poor Law* (Baltimore: The John Hopkins Press, 1969), p. 18.

56. Moynihan, *Maximum Feasible Misunderstanding*, p. 83.

57. William C. Selover, "The View from Capitol Hill," in James L. Sundquist and C.S. Schelling, eds., *On Fighting Poverty: Perspectives from Experience* (New York: Basic Books, 1969), p. 159.

58. Levitan, *The Great Society's Poor Law*, p. 46.

59. Ibid., p. 38.

60. Altshuler, *Community Control*, p. 184.

61. David C. Ranney, *Planning and Politics in the Metropolis* (Columbus: Merrill, 1969), p. 75.

62. Ibid.

63. Melvin B. Mogulof, *Citizen Participation: A Review and Commentary on Federal Policies and Practices* (Washington, D.C.: The Urban Institute, 1970), p. 63.

64. Sherry R. Arnstein, "Eight Rungs on the Ladder of Citizen Participation," in *Citizen Participation: Effecting Community Change*, Edgar S. Cahn and Barry A. Passett, eds. (New York: Praeger, 1971), p. 74.

65. Mogulof, *Citizen Participation*, p. 64.

66. See: Zimmerman, *The Federated City*, p. 5.

67. See: Moynihan, *Maximum Feasible Misunderstanding*, passim.

68. Levitan, *The Great Society's Poor Law*, p. 35.

69. Ibid., p. 36.

70. Moynihan, *Maximum Feasible Misunderstanding*, pp. 86-87.

71. Levitan, *The Great Society's Poor Law*, p. 44.

72. Moynihan, *Maximum Feasible Misunderstanding*, pp. 96-97.

73. Mogulof, *Citizen Participation*, p. 78.

74. For example see: Kenneth Clark and Jeannette Hopkins, *A Relevant War Against Poverty* (New York: Harper and Row, 1970), and Gary English, "The Trouble with Community Action," *Public Administration Review* 32 (May/June 1972), pp. 224-32.

75. Arnstein, "Eight Rungs on the Ladder of Citizen Participation," p. 75.

76. Ibid.

77. Zimmerman, *The Federated City*, p. 8.

78. Ibid., p. 9.

79. Mogulof, *Citizen Participation*, p. 69.

80. Arnstein, "Eight Rungs on the Ladder of Citizen Participation," p. 72.

81. Although not employed in the same manner as in this study, the dimension of scope also has been pointed out by: Yates, "Neighborhood Government," p. 212.

82. See: Mogulof, *Citizen Participation*, pp. 7-9 for a somewhat similar scheme.

83. Milton Kotler, *Neighborhood Government* (Indianapolis: Bobbs-Merrill, 1969). Although the East Central Citizens Organization did not begin as an OEO funded organization, at the time Kotler was writing his book ECCO was relying on OEO to meet most of its annual budget.

84. Mario Fantini, Marilyn Gittell, and Richard Magat, *Community Control and the Urban School* (New York: Praeger, 1970).

85. "Community Representation in 20 Cities," in Edgar S. Cahn and Barry A. Passett, eds., *Citizen Participation: Effecting Community Change* (New York: Praeger, 1971), pp. 200-214.

86. Washnis, *Neighborhood Facilities and Municipal Decentralization.*

87. Some observers do distinguish between territorial, administrative, and political patterns of decentralization. See, for example, Stenberg's, *The New Grass Roots Government?* Although such a scheme does improve upon the tendency to ignore important distinctions, it still represents only a very gross classification of citizen participation programs and is subject to many of the same criticisms outlined above.

88. Mogulof, *Citizen Participation*, p. 6.

89. Altshuler, *Community Control*, p. 44.

90. Yates, "Neighborhood Government," p. 212.

91. See Mogulof, *Citizen Participation*, pp. 4-6 for a description of others.

92. Yates, "Neighborhood Government," p. 212.

93. The distinction between inter- and intra-city comparisons is especially important when considering the *impact* of citizen involvement. As will be examined in Chapters 5 and 6, the impact of the various program structures, even *within* a city, may differ.

94. Mogulof, *Citizen Participation*, p. 12.

95. Schmandt, "Municipal Decentralization: An Overview," pp. 576 and 578.

96. Carl W. Stenberg, "Citizens and the Administrative State: From Participation to Power," *Public Administration Review* 32 (May/June 1972), p. 194.

97. Howard W. Hallman, *Community Corporations and Neighborhood Control* (Washington, D.C.: Center for Governmental Studies, 1970), p. 8.

98. Paul E. Peterson, "Forms of Representation: Participation of the Poor in the Community Action Programs," *The American Political Science Review* 64 (June 1970), pp. 491-508.

99. "Community Representation in 20 Cities," Cahn and Passett, eds., *Citizen Participation: Effecting Community Change*, pp. 200-214.

100. Stenberg, *The New Grass Roots Government?*

Chapter 2
Citizen Participation in American
Communities: An Analytical Scheme

1. The author wishes to express his appreciation to the International City Management Association and to the Advisory Commission on Intergovernmental Relations for making the results of this study available. A special note of acknowledgment is due Carl W. Stenberg, Service Analyst of the Advisory Commission Staff for his assistance and cooperation at a very crucial stage of this report. Of course, neitherof these organizations nor Mr. Stenberg are in any way responsible for the analysis herein presented.

2. Much of the research concerned with the voter turnout of such neighborhood elections and the representativeness of those selected to partici-pate in programs of neighborhood involvement is discussed in Chapters 5 and 6 of this study.

3. Carl W. Stenberg, *The New Grass Roots Government?* (Washington, D.C.: Advisory Commission on Intergovernmental Relations, 1972).

4. The author gratefully acknowledges the receipt of a David Ross Fellow-ship awarded by the Purdue Research Foundation, Purdue University, which made this phase of the research possible.

5. See: Hanna Pitkin, *The Concept of Representation* (Berkeley: University of California Press, 1967), and Paul E. Peterson, "Forms of Representation: Participation of the Poor in the Community Action Program," *The American Political Science Review* 64 (June 1970), pp. 491-507.

6. The categorization into these groups, it should be mentioned, is for purposes of convenience, only. Any number of groups could have been used, however the resulting sixteen cell matrix is a sufficient discriminator of programs for this analysis.

7. Claire Selltiz, Marie Jahoda, Morton Deutsch, and Stuart W. Cook, *Research Methods in Social Relations* (New York: Holt, Rinehart and Winston, 1962), pp. 359-66.

8. Ibid., pp. 369-70. Of course Selltiz et al. were concerned primarily with attitudinal scaling; however, the same principles appear applicable.

9. Robert L. Lineberry, and Edmund P. Fowler, "Reformism and Public Policies in American Cities," *American Political Science Review* 61 (September 1967), pp. 701-716.

10. *The Municipal Yearbook*, 1966 (Chicago: The International City Manage-ment Association,1966).

11. Robert L. Lineberry and Ira Sharkansky, *Urban Politics and Public Policy* (New York: Harper and Row, 1971), p. 169.

12. These data also are available in the 1966 *Municipal Yearbook.*

13. See Brett W. Hawkins, *Politics and Urban Policies* (Indianapolis: Bobbs-Merrill, 1971), pp. 44-47.

14. U.S., Congress, Senate, *Staff Study of Major Riots and Civil Disorders— 1965 through July 31, 1968*, prepared by the Permanent Subcommittee on Investigations of the Committee on Government Operations, 90th Cong., 2nd sess., 1968.

15. Ibid., pp. 1-2.

16. A complete discussion of the Guttman technique can be found in Selltiz et al., *Research Methods in Social Relations*, pp. 373-78.

17. For a description of stratified sampling, see: Bernard S. Phillips, *Social Research Strategy and Tactics* (New York: The MacMillan Company, 1969), pp. 267-68.

18. See: Raymond Wolfinger and John Field, "Political Ethos and the Structure of City Government," *American Political Science Review* 60 (June 1966), pp. 306-326.

19. A three-by-three matrix (resulting in nine cells) was relied upon in this instance simply because the data available lent themselves most readily to such a categorization. This index, also, is susceptible to the same sorts of criticisms reviews above (see page 51-54, Chapter 2).

20. Personal interview conducted with official of the city of Dayton, Ohio, December 11, 1972. Anonymity was assured all interviewees, therefore names and titles are omitted.

21. George J. Washnis, *Neighborhood Facilities and Municipal Decentralization* (Washington, D.C.: Center for Governmental Studies, 1971), p. 98.

22. Sherry R. Arnstein, "Eight Rungs on the Ladder of Citizen Participation," in *Citizen Participation: Effecting Community Change*, Edgar S. Cahn and Barry A. Passett, eds. (New York: Praeger, 1971), p. 85.

23. Personal interview conducted with official of the city of Indianapolis, Indiana, December 6, 1972.

24. James L. Sundquist and David W. Davis, *Making Federalism Work* (Washington, D.C.: The Brookings Institution, 1969), esp. chs. 1, 2, and 3.

25. Ibid., p. 46.

26. As quoted in Melvin B. Mogulof, *Citizen Participation: A Review and Commentary on Federal Policies and Practices* (Washington, D.C.: The Urban Institute, 1970), p. 65.

**Chapter 3
Citizen Participation and the
Urban Environment**

1. See Brett W. Hawkins, *Politics and Urban Policies* (Indianapolis: Bobbs-Merrill, 1971), pp. 12-14, for a similar analysis.

2. See David Easton, *The Political System: An Inquiry into the State of Political Science* (New York: Alfred A. Knopf, Inc., 1953).

3. Herbert Jacob and Michael Lipsky, "Outputs, Structure, and Power: An Assessment of Changes in the Study of State and Local Politics," in *Political Science*, Marian D. Irish, ed. (Englewood, New Jersey: Prentice-Hall, 1968), pp. 221-22.

4. Hawkins, *Politics and Urban Policies*, p. 8.

5. Raymond E. Wolfinger and John O. Field, "Political Ethos and the Structure of City Government," *American Political Science Review* 60 (June 1966), pp. 306-326.

6. Herbert Jacob, "The Consequences of Malapportionment: A Note of Caution," *Social Forces* 43 (1964), pp. 256-61.

7. Richard E. Dawson and James A. Robinson, "Interparty Competition, Economic Variables and Welfare Politics in the American States," *Journal of Politics* 25 (1963), pp. 265-89.

8. See Jacob and Lipsky, "Outputs, Structure, and Power," for an elaboration of these criticisms.

9. Wolfinger and Field, "Political Ethos and the Structure of City Government," pp. 306-326.

10. Robert L. Lineberry and Edmund P. Fowler, "Reformism and Public Policies in American Cities," *American Political Science Review*, 61 (September 1967), pp. 701-716.

11. William R. Shaffer and Ronald E. Weber, "Policy Responsiveness in the American States," paper delivered at the 1972 American Political Science Association meeting in Washington, D.C., p. 1.

12. Ronald E. Weber and William R. Shaffer, "Public Opinion and American State Policy-Making," paper delivered at the 1970 meeting of the Midwest Political Science Association in Chicago, Ill. It should be mentioned that Weber and Shaffer were principally interested in the effect of public opinion on policy.

13. One obvious complicating factor in examining citizen participation from this perspective is that the policy undoubtedly is heavily influenced by federal-funding requirements. Thus one might suspect that the only factor of significance would be whether or not the city had accepted federal funds which required citizen input in their expenditure. There is no doubt, as will be demonstrated below, that federal-funding requirements have had a tremendous impact on citizen participation activities. Nevertheless, federal mandates clearly are not the *only* factors influencing the adoption of citizen participation programs since (as will be shown below) almost 25 percent of those cities receiving no federal funds have adopted some form of participation program. However, the most important point to be made here is, as the reader will recall, that what is being examined in this study is not simply whether a city has adopted a citizen participation program; rather, it is that city's ranking on the index of citizen involvement which accounts for both intensity of citizen

participation and variety of program adopted which is of primary concern. Thus, it is argued, two cities receiving the same amount of money from the same federal-funding source (say, OEO) could construct widely different structures of participation activities. One might encourage a great deal of "meaningful" citizen input, in the other only token involvement might be tolerated. The index of participation constructed for this study should be sensitive to these variances and, of course, it is these differences being examined in Chapters 3 and 4.

14. The author is indebted to William R. Shaffer for pointing out this omission.

15. For a full discussion of this problem see: James J. Noell's "Letter to the Editor," appearing in the *American Political Science Review* 64 (December 1970), pp. 1249-51; and John L. Sullivan, "A Note on Redistributive Politics," *American Political Science Review* 66 (December 1972), pp. 1301-1306.

16. A concern with cultural influences on politics is, of course, not unique to students of urban politics. See: Daniel J. Elazar, *American Federalism: A View from the States* (New York: Thomas Y. Crowell, 1966), and Gabriel A. Almond and Sidney Verba, *The Civic Culture* (Boston: Little, Brown and Company, 1963) for cultural applications at the state and cross-national levels.

17. See: Edward C. Banfield and James Q. Wilson, *City Politics* (Cambridge, Mass.: Harvard University Press, 1963), and James Q. Wilson and Edward C. Banfield, "Public Regardingness as a Value Premise in Voting Behavior," *American Political Science Review* 58 (December 1964), pp. 876-87.

18. As interpreted by Robert L. Lineberry and Ira Sharkansky, *Urban Politics and Public Policy* (New York: Harper and Row, 1971), p. 72.

19. Banfield and Wilson, *City Politics*, p. 46 (emphasis mine).

20. Richard Hofstadter, *The Age of Reform* (New York: Alfred A. Knopf, 1955), p. 9.

21. Richard Binstock, *A Report On Politics in Worcester, Massachusetts* (Cambridge: Joint Center of Urban Studies, 1961), p. 2.

22. See: Edgar Litt, "Jewish Ethno-Religious Involvement and Political Liberalism," *Social Forces* (May 1961), pp. 328-32; and Edgar Litt, "Ethnic Status and Political Perspectives," *Midwest Journal of Political Science* (August 1961), pp. 276-83.

23. Banfield and Wilson, *City Politics*, p. 330.

24. John Kessel, "Governmental Structure and Political Environment: A Statistical Note about American Cities," *American Political Science Review* (September 1962), pp. 615-20.

25. Edgar Sherbenou, "Class, Participation, and the Council-Manager Plan," *Public Administration Review* 21 (Summer 1961), pp. 131-35.

26. Leo Schnore and Robert Alford, "Forms of Government and Socio-economic Characteristics of Suburbs," *Administrative Science Quarterly* 7 (June 1963), pp. 1-17.

27. Ibid.

28. Robert Alford and Harry Scoble, "Political and Socioeconomic Characteristics of Cities," *The Municipal Year Book, 1965* (Chicago: The International City Management Association, 1965), pp. 82-97.

29. Schnore and Alford, "Forms of Government and Socio-economic Characteristics of Suburbs."

30. Ibid.

31. Wolfinger and Field, "Political Ethos and the Structure of City Government."

32. Carl W. Stenberg, "Citizens and the Administrative State: From Participation to Power," *Public Administration Review* 32 (May/June 1972), p. 190 (emphasis mine).

33. Joseph F. Zimmerman, *The Federated City* (New York: St. Martin's Press, 1972), p. 16.

34. Alan A. Altshuler, *Community Control* (New York: Pegasus, 1970), p. 18.

35. As mentioned in Chapter 2, the source of information for the construction of this index was supplied by the Advisory Commission on Intergovernmental Relations (based upon its 1970 survey of all cities in the United States) and the International City Management Association.

36. David M. Austin, "Resident Participation: Political Mobilization or Organizational Co-optation?" *Public Administration Review* 32 (September 1972), p. 416.

37. Carl W. Stenberg, *The New Grass Roots Government?* (Advisory Commission on Intergovernmental Relations: Washington, D.C., 1972), p. 4.

38. Banfield and Wilson, *City Politics*, p. 183.

39. Robert C. Wood, *Suburbia* (Boston: Houghton Mifflin Company, 1958), p. 13.

40. Ibid., p. 153.

41. Ibid., p. 157.

42. Wolfinger and Field, "Political Ethos and the Structure of City Government."

43. Ibid.

44. Stenberg, *The New Grass Roots Government?*, p. 3.

45. Wilson and Banfield, "Public Regardingness as a Value Premise in Voting Behavior," p. 885.

46. Alford and Scoble, "Characteristics of American Cities," pp. 93-96.

47. As reported in Hawkins, *Politics and Urban Politics*, pp. 21-23.

48. Lineberry and Fowler, "Reformism and Public Policies in American Cities."

49. Edward C. Banfield, *The Un-Heavenly City* (Boston: Little, Brown and Company, 1968), p. 64.

50. See: Alford and Scoble, "Political and Socio-economic Characteristics of Cities"; Wolfinger and Field, "Political Ethos and the Structure of City

Government"; and Lineberry and Fowler, "Reformism and Public Policies in American Cities," for examples of other studies using these same measures of social class.

51. Banfield and Wilson, it should be noted, seem to consider "class" simply in terms of income. They state, "In thecity, it is useful to think in terms of three income groups—low, middle, and high. The poorest people favor a high level of expenditures.... Upper income people also favor a high level of expenditures. The middle-income group generally wants a low level of public expenditures." In, *City Politics*, pp. 35-36. Of course, the measure of "medium income" employed here encompasses this definition of class.

52. Lineberry and Fowler, "Reformism and Public Policies in American Cities."

53. Douglas Yates, "Neighborhood Government," *Policy Sciences* 3 (July 1972), pp. 209-219.

54. Austin, "Resident Participation: Political Mobilization or Organizational Co-optation?"

55. Altshuler, *Community Control*, p. 16 (emphasis mine).

56. Ibid., p. 191.

Chapter 4
Citizen Participation and
Urban Politics

1. Brett W. Hawkins, *Politics and Urban Policies* (Indianapolis: Bobbs-Merrill, 1971), p. 85.

2. Ibid., p. 94.

3. Ibid.

4. Ibid., p. 45.

5. All data concerning the number of local governments per area and population were taken from the *United States Census of Governments*.

6. This is essentially the argument made by: Robert L. Lineberry and Edmund P. Fowler in, "Reformism and Public Policies in American Cities," *American Political Science Review* 61 (September 1967), pp. 701-716.

7. Those interested in this debate might wish to review the exchange between Lineberry/Fowler and Wolfinger/Field which appeared in the "Communications" section of the *American Political Science Review* 62 (March 1968), pp. 227-231.

8. William G. Scott, "Organization Government: The Prospects for a Truly Participative System," *Public Administration Review* 29 (January/February 1969), pp. 43-53.

9. Adam W. Herbert, "Management under Conditions of Decentralization and Citizen Participation" *Public Administration Review* 32 (October 1972), pp. 622-38.

10. Ibid., p. 624.

11. Alan A. Altshuler, *Community Control* (New York: Pegasus, 1970), p. 107.

12. Joseph F. Zimmerman, "Neighborhoods and Citizen Involvement," *Public Administration Review*, 32 (May/June 1972), pp. 201-09.

13. Lineberry and Fowler, "Reformism and Public Policies in American Cities," p. 715.

14. Robert C. Wood, "The Contributions of Political Science to Urban Form," in *Urban Life and Form*, Werner Z. Hirsch eds. (New York: Holt, Rinehart, and Winston, 1963), p. 100.

15. Edward C. Banfield, *Political Influence* (New York: Free Press, 1961), p. 237.

16. Herbert Kaufman, "Administrative Decentralization and Political Power," paper presented at the meeting of the American Political Science Association, September 1968, pp. 12-13.

17. Altshuler, *Community Control*, p. 112.

18. James Q. Wilson, "Planning and Politics: Citizen Participation in Urban Renewal," in *Urban Renewal: People, Politics and Planning*, Jewel Bellush and Murray Hausknecht, eds. (New York: Doubleday, 1967), p. 299.

19. Zimmerman, "Neighborhoods and Citizen Involvement," pp. 201-09.

20. All measures of mayoralty strength were taken from: *The Municipal Year Book, 1966* (Chicago: The International City Management Association, 1966).

21. Daniel M. Fox, "Federal Standards and Regulations for Participation," in *Citizen Participation: Effecting Community Change*, Edgar S. Cahn and Barry A. Passett, eds. (New York: Praeger, 1971), p. 139 (emphasis mine).

22. Because the ACIR survey of citizen participation programs did not solicit information which would allow an estimation of the date of program adoption, it is impossible to draw causal inferences from these findings. However, at least one observer has found that the surge of "interest in neighborhood government gained impetus *following* the civil disorders of the mid 1960's" (see: Joseph F. Zimmerman, *The Federated City*—New York: St. Martin's Press, 1972—p. 1). It seems reasonable to assume, then, that at least a significant proportion of those citizen participation activities reported in the ACIR survey were initiated in response to urban violence.

23. Suzanne Farkas, "The Federal Role in Urban Decentralization," *American Behavioral Scientist* 15 (September/October 1971), pp. 15-36.

24. Information on these various programs was gathered from the following official publications: For Urban Renewal Funds, the *Urban Renewal Directory* (Washington, D.C.: U.S. Department of Housing and Urban Development, December 31, 1971); for OEO funds, the *Community Action Agency Atlas* (Washington, D.C.: Office of Economic Opportunity, May 1971); and for Model Cities Funds, the *HUD NEWS* (Washington, D.C.: Department of Housing and Urban Development, September 21, 1972). The author is grateful to these various agencies for supplying these pamphlets.

25. As reported in the *Congressional Quarterly Weekly* (Washington, D.C.: Congressional Quarterly, April 21, 1973), p. 907.

26. The text of the president's speech is found in the *Congressional Quarterly Almanac* (Washington, D.C.: Congressional Quarterly, 1971), p. 63-A.

27. As reported in the *Congressional Quarterly Weekly Report* (Washington, D.C.: Congressional Quarterly, March 10, 1973), p. 506.

28. Ibid., March 3, 1973, p. 431.

29. Henry J. Schmandt, "Municipal Decentralization: An Overview," *Public Administration Review* 32 (October 1972), p. 584.

30. See: James J. Noell's "Letter to the Editor," appearing in the December, 1970 issue of the *American Political Science Review*, pp. 1249-50.

31. Robert A. Gordon, "Issues in Multiple Regression," *American Journal of Sociology* 73 (1968), pp. 592-616.

32. One might argue, of course, that this process imposes an element of artificiality on the data since in the real world these variables may overlap. It is only suggested here that the elimination of the problem of multicollinearity by this method is worth this risk.

33. The reader will note that a few variables not examined above (such as median age and employment status) are allowed to enter into this factor routine. Although the significance of these variables to the participation movement were not previously tested, they are also measures of the urban social and political condition and deserve to be considered when attempting to discover the important dimensions of the urban environment.

34. Robert A. Dahl, "The City in the Future of Democracy," *American Political Science Review* 61 (December 1967), pp. 953-71.

35. See the discussion of the sociological perspective of citizen participation presented in Chapter 1 of this study.

36. Raymond E. Wolfinger and John O. Field, "Political Ethos and the Structure of City Government," *American Political Science Review* 60 (June 1966), pp. 325-26.

37. Hawkins, *Politics and Urban Policies*, p. 85.

38. For an initial attempt to assess the impact of leadership styles on the urban policy process see: Robert Eyestone, *The Threads of Public Policy: A Study in Policy Leadership* (Indianapolis: Bobbs-Merrill Company, 1971).

39. Robert Lineberry and Ira Sharkansky (*Urban Politics and Public Policy*, New York: Harper and Row, 1971) have provided a catalog of a variety of factors which may affect municipal spending levels. Among those governmental variables which they mention are the following: state-local centralization; intergovernmental aid; state debt and expenditure limits; previous expenditures; participation in local politics; and party competition. A complete model of the urban policy process, it seems, would need to incorporate the effects of these, and other influences.

40. A similar conclusion was reached in: Richard L. Cole, "The Urban Policy Process: A Note on Structural and Regional Influences," *Social Science Quarterly* 52 (December 1971), pp. 646-56.

Chapter 5
Participant Motives and Descriptive
Characteristics

1. Charles O. Jones, *An Introduction to the Study of Public Policy* (Belmont, California: Duxbury Press, 1970), p. 107.

2. Ibid., p. 109.

3. Ronald E. Weber and William R. Shaffer, "The Costs and Benefits of American State-Local Government Policies," paper delivered at the Annual meeting of the *Southwestern Political Science Association*, San Antonio, Texas, March 30-April 1, 1972.

4. See, for example, the symposium entitled "Neighborhoods and Citizen Involvement" published in the 1972 May/June issue of the *Public Administration Review*, pp. 189-224.

5. See: Sherry Arnstein, "Maximum Feasible Manipulation," *Public Administration Review* 32 (September 1972), pp. 377-390; Milton Kotler, *Neighborhood Government* (Indianapolis: Bobbs-Merrill, 1969); and Kenneth Clark and Jeannette Hopkins, *A Relevant War against Poverty* (New York: Harper and Row, 1968).

6. See: Ralph M. Kramer, *Participation of the Poor* (Englewood Cliffs, New Jersey: Prentice-Hall, 1969), p. 256.

7. Ibid., (emphasis mine).

8. Henry J. Schmandt, "Municipal Decentralization: An Overview," *Public Administration Review* 32 (October 1972), p. 578.

9. Paul E. Peterson, "Forms of Representation: Participation of the Poor in the Community Action Program," *The American Political Science Review* 64 (June 1970), pp. 491-508.

10. Jon Van Till and Sally Van Till, "Citizen Participation in the Social Policy: The End of the Cycle?" *Social Problems* 17 (1969-1970), pp. 313-23.

11. See James Q. Wilson, "Planning and Politics: Citizen Participation in Urban Renewal," in *Urban Renewal: People, Politics and Planning*, Jewel Bellush and Murray Hausknecht, eds. (New York: Doubleday, 1967), p. 299.

12. Peterson, "Forms of Representation."

13. Neil Gilbert, *Clients or Constituents* (San Francisco: Josey-Bass, 1970), p. 35.

14. David A. Caputo, "Evaluating Urban Public Policy: A Developmental Model and Some Reservations," *Public Administration Review* 33 (March/April 1973), pp. 113-19.

15. See: Carl Stenberg, *The New Grass Roots Government?* (Washington, D.C.: Advisory Commission on Intergovernmental Relations, 1972).

16. Melvin Mogulof, *Citizen Participation: A Review and Commentary on Federal Policies and Practices* (Washington, D.C.: The Urban Institute, 1970), p. 105.

17. Robert Alford and Eugene Lee, "Votir̶ ̶ ̶ ̶ ̶ ̶ ̶ ̶ ̶ A̶ ̶ ̶ ̶ ̶ ̶ ̶ ̶"
American Political Science Review 62 (Septer̶ ̶ ̶ ̶ ̶ ̶ ̶ ̶ ̶ ̶ ̶ ̶ ̶ ̶ ̶

18. Edgar L. Sherbenou, "Class, Par̶ ̶ ̶ ̶ ̶ ̶ ̶ ̶ ̶ ̶ ̶ ̶ ̶ .ager
Plan," *Public Administration Review* 21̶ ̶

19. Amos H. Hawley, "Commur̶ success,"
American Journal of Sociology 68 (̶

20. Stanley Liberson and ̶A̶ .ecipitants and
Underlying Conditions of R̶ gical Review̶, 30
(December 1965), pp. 887-9̶

21. Peter Eisinger, "T̶'̶ ̶r in American Cities,"
*American Political Science̶ ̶. 11-29.

22. Ibid., p. 12.

23. Alan Altshuler, *Commun̶.̶ ̶ ̶ ̶ ̶ ̶ ̶ ̶ ̶ ̶ ̶* York: Pegasus, 1970), p. 18.

24. Schmandt, "Municipal Decen̶t̶.̶ ̶ ̶ ̶ ̶ ̶ An Overview," p. 578.

25. Altshuler, *Community Control*, p̶ ̶ ̶ ̶ ̶ ̶.

26. Arnstein, "Maximum Feasible Manipulation," p. 389.

27. James J. Vanecko, "Community Mobilization and Institutional Change,"
Social Science Quarterly 50 (December 1969), pp. 609-631.

28. Clark and Hopkins, *A Relevant War against Poverty*, p. 65.

29. Gilbert, *Clients or Constituents* pp. 155-56.

30. Ibid.

31. Schmandt, "Municipal Decentralization: An Overview," p. 584.

32. Vanecko, "Community Mobilization and Institutional Change," p. 629.

33. Kramer, *Participation of the Poor*, p. 184.

34. Many of these studies are presented in the following section. However,
for an introduction to this sort of analysis, one might consult: Robert A. Dahl,
Who Governs? (New Haven Yale University Press, 1961), esp. Ch. 26, pp.
282-301.

35. Hannah Pitkin, *The Concept of Representation* (Berkeley: University of
California Press, 1967), p. 61.

36. J.C. Bluntshli as quoted in Pitkin, *The Concept of Representation*, p. 62.

37. Ibid., p. 64.

38. See the exchange between neighborhood participants and local officials
concerning the representation on the Philadelphia Model Cities board in: *Public
Administration Review* 32 (September 1972), pp. 377-402.

39. Lester Milbrath, *Political Participation* (Chicago: Rand McNally, 1965),
p. 110 (emphasis mine).

40. Donald R. Matthews, *The Social Background of Political Decision-Makers*
(Garden City, New York: Doubleday and Company, 1954).

41. Morris Axelrod, "Urban Structure and Social Participation," *American
Sociological Review* 21 (February 1956), pp. 13-38.

42. John C. Bollens, ed., *Exploring the Metropolitan Community*, (Berkeley:
University of California Press, 1961).

43. Charles Bonjean, "Mass, Class, and the Industrial Community: A Comparative Analysis of Managers, Businessmen and Workers," *American Journal of Sociology* 72 (September 1966), pp. 149-62.

44. Basil Zimmer and Amos Hawley, "The Significance of Membership in Associations," *American Journal of Sociology* 65 (September 1959), pp. 196-220.

45. Eustice Theodore and Carol Theodore, "Citizen Awareness and Involvement in Poverty Action," *Social Problems* 19 (Spring 1972), pp. 484-96.

46. Gilbert, *Clients or Constituents*, p. 150.

47. Walter Grove and Herbert Costner, "Organizing the Poor: An Evaluation of a Strategy," *Social Science Quarterly* 50 (December 1969), pp. 643-57.

48. Gilbert, *Clients or Constituents*, see esp. Ch. 2.

49. This information was obtained from: U.S. Bureau of the Census, *Census of Population and Housing: 1970, CENSUS TRACTS* (Washington, D.C.: U.S. Government Printing Office, 1972). In one instance, the analysis reported in this section was not possible since one city, Richmond, is not included in the census tract publications.

50. Obviously, the construction of such a composite score ignores individual differences within each category. However, it is this composite relationship which is of particular interest here.

51. Gilbert, *Clients or Constituents*, p. 158.

52. Charles Hyneman, "Who Makes Our Laws?" *Political Science Quarterly* 55 (December 1940), pp. 556-81.

53. Pitkin, *The Concept of Representation*, p. 89.

54. Gilbert, *Clients or Constituents*, p. 158.

55. Altshuler, *Community Control*, p. 45.

56. Peterson, "Forms of Representation," p. 501.

Chapter 6
Neighborhood Involvement,
Participant Satisfaction,
and Citizen Trust

1. See: Ch. 1 of this study, the section, "Citizen Participation, Urban Disorders, and the Delivery of Municipal Services."

2. Henry J. Schmandt, "Municipal Decentralization: An Overview," *Public Administration Review* 32 (October 1972), pp. 576, 578.

3. Douglas Yates, "Neighborhood Government," *Policy Sciences* 2 (July 1972), p. 213.

4. Joseph F. Zimmerman, *The Federated City* (New York: St. Martin's Press, 1972), p. 15.

5. Robert L. Bish, *The Public Economy of Metropolitan Areas*, (Chicago: Markham, 1971).

6. Ibid., p. 49.

7. Alan A. Altshuler, *Community Control* (New York: Pegasus, 1970), p. 47.

8. Joel D. Aberbach and Jack L. Walker, "Political Trust and Racial Ideology," *The American Political Science Review* 64 (December 1970), pp. 1199-1220.

9. Lynne B. Iglitzin, *Violent Conflict in American Society* (San Francisco: Chandler Publishing Company, 1972), p. 48.

10. Robert A. Dahl, *Polyarchy* (New Haven: Yale University Press, 1971), pp. 150-53.

11. William A. Gamson, *Power and Discontent* (Homewood, Illinois: The Dorsey Press, 1968).

12. Ibid., p. 83.

13. For an expanded version of this model see: Richard L. Cole, "Toward a Model of Political Trust: A Causal Analysis," *Midwest Journal of Political Science* (February 1973), forthcoming.

14. Aberbach and Walker, "Political Trust and Racial Ideology," p. 1243.

15. See also: Richard L. Cole, "On the Causes and Consequences of Political Trust: A Causal Analysis," presented at the annual meeting of the *Midwest Political Science Association*, April 28, 1972.

16. Peter Eisinger, "The Conditions of Protest Behavior in American Cities," *American Political Science Review* 67 (March 1973), pp. 11-29.

17. George Washnis, *Neighborhood Facilities and Municipal Decentralization* (Washington, D.C.: Center for Governmental Studies, 1971), pp. 62-63.

18. Louis A. Zurcher, "The Poverty Board: Some Consequences of 'Maximum Feasible Participation,'" *Journal of Social Issues* 26 (Summer 1970), pp. 85-107.

19. John H. Strange, "The Impact of Citizen Participation on Public Administration," *Public Administration Review* 32 (September 1972), pp. 457-70.

20. Washnis, *Neighborhood Facilities and Municipal Decentralization*, p. 63.

21. Neil Gilbert, *Clients or Constituents* (San Francisco: Josey-Bass, 1970), p. 164.

22. Willis A. Sutton, "Differential Perceptions of Impact of a Rural Anti-Poverty Campaign," *Social Science Quarterly* 50 (December 1969), pp. 662.

23. Peter H. Rossi, "No Good Idea Goes Unpublished," *Social Science Quarterly*, 50 (December 1969), p. 473.

24. Yates, "Neighborhood Government," p. 212.

25. Sherry Arnstein, "Eight Rungs on the Ladder of Citizen Participation," in *Citizen Participation: Effecting Community Change*, Edgar S. Cahn and Barry Passett (New York: Praeger, 1971), p. 72.

26. *Report of the National Advisory Commission on Civil Disorders* (New York: Bantam Books, 1968), p. 203.

27. Ibid., p. 205.

28. Ibid., p. 289, 297.

29. Aberbach and Walker, "Political Trust and Racial Ideology," p. 1218.

30. For a discussion and elaboration of these trust items and the resulting trust scale, see: John P. Robinson, Jerrold G. Rusk, and Kendra B. Head, *Measures of Political Attitudes* (Ann Arbor, Michigan: Institute for Social Research, 1968), pp. 633, 643-46.

31. This relationship was maintained when controlling for race.

32. Herbert H. Hyman, *Secondary Analysis of Sample Surveys* (New York: John Wiley and Sons, 1972), p. 35.

33. Ibid., p. 66.

34. Ibid., pp. 62-69.

35. It has been found that race is an extremely important variable in discriminating among partisan trust scores. See: Cole, "On the Causes and Consequences of Political Trust."

36. When the combined "Scale of Political Trust" is examined the same results are observed.

37. William Erbe, "Social Involvement and Political Activity," *American Sociological Review* 29 (April 1964), pp. 198-215.

38. For a more complete explanation of this thesis see: Ted Gurr, "A Causal Model of Civil Strife: A Comparative Analysis," *American Political Science Review* 62 (1968), pp. 1104-1125 and James C. Davies, "Toward A Theory of Revolution," *The American Sociological Review* 27 (February 1962), pp. 5-19.

39. As quoted in Davies, "Toward a Theory of Revolution," p. 5.

40. *Report of the National Advisory Commission on Civil Disorders*, pp. 226-227.

41. Personal interview conducted with official of the City of Dayton, Ohio, December 11, 1972.

42. Paul E. Peterson, "Forms of Representation: Participation of the Poor in the Community Action Program," *The American Political Science Review* 64 (June 1970), pp. 491-508.

43. Ibid., p. 500.

44. Michael Lipsky, "Protest as a Political Resource," *American Political Science Review* 62 (December 1968), pp. 1144-58.

45. Ibid., p. 1158.

46. James L. Sundquist and David W. Davis, *Making Federalism Work* (Washington, D.C.: The Brookings Institution, 1969), pp. 46 and 117.

47. Ibid., p. 116.

48. Ibid., p. 45.

49. Ibid., p. 67.

50. Ibid., p. 45.

50. Ibid., p. 118.

52. Howard W. Hallman, "Federally Financed Citizen Participation," *Public Administration Review* 32 (September 1972), pp. 421-28.

Chapter 7
Conclusion: Policy and
Theoretical Implications

1. Daniel C. Kramer, *Participatory Democracy: Developing Ideals of the Political Left* (Cambridge, Massachusetts: Schenkman Publishing Company, 1972), p. 10-13.

2. Ibid., p. 15.

3. Ibid., p. 16.

4. A thorough discussion of the European work council, and especially its operation in Yugoslavia, can be found in: Carole Pateman, *Participation and Democratic Theory* (Cambridge: Cambridge University Press, 1970).

5. See the comparison of the case-study and comparative approaches presented in: Arend Lijphart, "Comparative Politics and the Comparative Model," *American Political Science Review* 65 (September 1971), pp. 682-94.

6. See: Raymond E. Wolfinger and John O. Field, "Political Ethos and the Structure of City Government," *American Political Science Review* 60 (June 1966), pp. 306-326; and Richard L. Cole, "The Urban Policy Process: A Note on Structural and Regional Influences," *Social Science Quarterly* 52 (December 1971), pp. 646-56. One area of interest which might be pursued is the difference between black and white attitudes in the United States and the degree to which these attitudes might be considered as cultural distinctions.

7. James L. Sundquist and David W. Davis, *Making Federalism Work* (Washington, D.C.: The Brookings Institution, 1969), p. 10.

8. William R. Shaffer, "Dimensions of Political Culture in the American States," unpublished manuscript.

9. Sundquist and David, *Making Federalism Work*, p. 10.

10. Ibid., pp. 3-4.

11. Michael D. Reagan, *The New Federalism* (New York: Oxford University Press, 1972), pp. 31-32.

12. Ibid., p. 59.

13. A brief review of these can be found in: Peter K. Eisinger, "The Conditions of Protest Behavior in American Cities," *The American Political Science Review* 67 (March 1973), pp. 11-28.

14. See: Gabriel A. Almond and G. Bingham Powell, *Comparative Politics, A Developmental Approach* (Boston: Little, Brown and Company, 1966), p. 65.

15. For a representative sample of these see: Kenneth P. Langton, *Political Socialization* (New York: Oxford Press, 1969); Fred Greenstein, *Children and Politics* (New Haven: Yale University Press, 1965); David Easton and Jack Dennis, "The Child's Acquisition of Regime Norms: Political Efficacy," *American Political Science Review* 61 (March 1967), pp. 25-38; and David Easton and Robert Hess, "The Child's Political World," *Midwest Journal of Political Science* 6 (August 1962), pp. 229-46.

16. Dale Rogers Marshall, *The Politics of Participation in Poverty* (Berkeley: University of California Press, 1971), p. 145.

17. Peter Marris and Martin Rein, *Dilemmas of Social Reform* (Chicago: Aldine Publishing Company, 1967), p. 220.

18. Pateman, *Participation and Democratic Theory*, p. 104.

19. Ibid., p. 46.

20. Angus Campbell, Gerald Gurin, and Warren Miller, *The Voter Decides* (Evanston, Illinois: Row, Peterson and Company, 1954), p. 187.

21. Angus Campbell, Philip Converse, Warren Miller, and Donald Stokes, *The American Voter* (New York: John Wiley, 1964), p. 58.

22. Pateman, *Participation and Democratic Theory*, p. 46.

23. Kramer, *Participatory Democracy*, p. 222 (emphasis mine).

24. For an explanation of this scale see: John P. Robinson, Jerrold G. Rusk, and Kendra B. Head, *Measures of Political Attitudes* (Ann Arbor: Institute for Social Research, 1968), pp. 459-61.

25. For a discussion of many of these studies see: Lester W. Milbrath, *Political Participation* (Chicago: Rand McNally, 1971), p. 63.

26. Marshall, *The Politics of Participation in Poverty*, p. 107.

27. Pateman, *Participation and Democratic Theory*, p. 66.

28. Personal interview conducted December 14, 1972.

29. Personal interview conducted November 21, 1972.

30. Personal interview conducted December 6, 1972.

31. It should be remembered that these meetings were all visited during the winter months and this obviously may have affected attendance records.

32. These, and other statistics revealing similar results, are available in Kramer, *Participatory Democracy*, pp. 76-107.

33. Sherry R. Arnstein, "Maximum Feasible Manipulation," *Public Administration Review* 32 (September 1972), p. 389.

34. Kramer, *Participatory Democracy*, p. 107.

35. Ibid., pp. 222 and 213.

36. Peter Bachrach, *The Theory of Democratic Elitism* (Boston: Little, Brown and Company, 1967), p. 103.

37. Pateman, *Participation and Democratic Theory*, p. 102.

38. Pateman briefly reviews a number of possible options including the family and the school.

39. This information was gathered from: *The Urban Renewal Directory* (Washington, D.C.: U.S. Department of Housing and Urban Development, December 31, 1971); the *Community Action Agency Atlas* (Washington, D.C.: Office of Economic Opportunity, May 1971); the *HUD NEWS* (Washington, D.C.: Department of Housing and Urban Development, September 21, 1972).

40. For a review of some of these sources see: *Making Democracy Work* (National Federation of Settlements and Neighborhood Centers: New York, 1966).

41. An interesting appraisal of the worth of such investigations is presented in: Arnstein, "Maximum Feasible Manipulation."

42. One exception to this is: Willis A. Sutton, "Differential Perceptions of Impact of a Rural Anti-Poverty Campaign," *Social Science Quarterly* 50 (December 1969), pp. 657-68.

43. Reported in: "Community Representation in 20 Cities," in *Citizen Participation: Effecting Community Change*, Edgar S. Cahn and Barry A. Passett, eds. (New York: Praeger, 1971), pp. 200-214.

44. See Pateman, *Participation and Democratic Theory*, pp. 108-109 for a brief review of some of these.

45. Kramer, *Participatory Democracy*, p. 225.

46. David Easton, *A Systems Analysis of Political Life* (New York: John Wiley, 1965), p. 273.

47. William A. Gamson, *Power and Discontent* (Homewood, Illinois: The Dorsey Press, 1968), p. 46.

48. James Q. Wilson, "Planning and Politics: Citizen Participation in Urban Renewal," in *Urban Renewal: People, Politics and Planning*, Jewel Bellush and Murray Hausknecht, eds. (New York: Doubleday, 1967), p. 299.

49. Ira Katznelson, "Antagonistic Ambiguity: Notes on Reformism and Decentralization," *Politics and Society* 3 (Spring 1972), pp. 328, 333.

50. Personal interview conducted November 21, 1972.

51. Kramer, *Participatory Democracy*, pp. 216-17.

52. Ibid., p. 217-18.

53. Ibid., p. 222.

54. Kenneth Clark and Jeannette Hopkins, *A Relevant War Against Poverty* (New York: Harper and Row, 1968), p. 256.

55. Henry Schmandt, "Municipal Decentralization: An Overview," *Public Administration Review* 32 (October 1972), p. 584.

Bibliography

Bibliography

Aberbach, Joel D., and Jack L. Walker, "Political Trust and Racial Ideology," *The American Political Science Review* 64 (December 1970), pp. 1199-1220.

Aleshire, Robert A., "Planning and Citizen Participation," *Urban Affairs Quarterly* 5 (1969-1970), pp. 370-93.

Alford, Robert, and Harry Scoble, "Political and Socio-economic Characteristics of Cities," *The Municipal Year Book, 1965* (Chicago: The International City Management Association, 1965), pp. 82-97.

_____, and Eugene Lee, "Voting Turnout in American Cities," *American Political Science Review* 62 (September 1968), pp. 796-813.

Almond, Gabriel A., and Sidney Verba, *The Civic Culture* (Boston: Little, Brown and Company, 1963).

_____, and G. Bingham Powell, *Comparative Politics, A Developmental Approach* (Boston: Little, Brown and Company, 1966).

Altshuler, Alan A., *Community Control* (New York: Pegasus, 1970).

Arnstein, Sherry R., "Eight Rungs on the Ladder of Citizen Participation," in *Citizen Participation: Effecting Community Change*, Edgar S. Cahn and Barry A. Passett, eds. (New York: Praeger, 1971).

Aron, Raymond, "Social Structure and the Ruling Class," *British Journal of Sociology* 1 (1950), pp. 1-16.

Austin, David M., "Resident Participation: Political Mobilization or Organizational Co-optation?" *Public Administration Review* 32 (September 1972), pp. 409-21.

Axelrod, Morris, "Urban Structure and Social Participation," *American Sociological Review* 21 (February 1956), pp. 13-18.

Bachrach, Peter, *The Theories of Democratic Elitism* (Boston: Little, Brown and Company, 1967).

Banfield, Edward, and James Q. Wilson, *Political Influence* (New York: Free Press, 1961).

_____, *City Politics* (Cambridge, Mass.: Harvard University Press, 1963).

_____, *The Un-Heavenly City* (Boston: Little, Brown and Company, 1968).

Bell, Daniel, *The End of Ideology* (Glencoe, Illinois: The Free Press, 1960).

Berelson, Bernard, Paul F. Lazarsfeld, and William McPhee, *Voting* (Chicago: University of Chicago Press, 1954).

Binstock, Richard, *A Report on Politics in Worcester, Massachusetts* (Cambridge: Joint Center of Urban Studies, 1961).

Bish, Robert L., *The Public Economy of Metropolitan Areas* (Chicago: Markham, 1971).

Bollens, John C., ed., *Exploring the Metropolitan Community* (Berkeley: University of California Press, 1961).

Bonjean, Charles, "Mass, Class, and the Industrial Community," *American Journal of Sociology* 72 (September 1966), pp. 149-62.

165

Brooks, Wendy Goepel, "Health Care and Poor People," in *Citizen Participation: Effecting Community Change*, Edgar S. Cahn and Barry A. Passett, eds. (New York: Praeger, 1971).

Campbell, Angus, Gerald Gurin, and Warren Miller, *The Voter Decides* (Evanston, Illinois: Row, Peterson and Company, 1954).

Caputo, David A., "Evaluating Urban Public Policy: A Developmental Model and Some Reservations," *Public Administration Review* 33 (March/April 1973), pp. 113-19.

Clark, Kenneth, and Jeannette Hopkins, *A Relevant War Against Poverty* (New York: Harper and Row, 1970).

Cole, Richard L., "The Urban Policy Process: A Note on Structural and Regional Influence," *Social Science Quarterly* 52 (December 1971), pp. 646-56.

————, "On the Causes and Consequences of Political Trust: A Causal Analysis," presented at the annual meeting of the Midwest Political Science Association, April 28, 1972.

————, "Toward a Model of Political Trust: A Causal Analysis," *Midwest Journal of Political Science* (February 1973), forthcoming.

Community Action Agency Atlas (Washington, D.C.: Office of Economic Opportunity, May 1971).

Dahl, Robert A., *A Preface to Democratic Theory* (Chicago: University of Chicago Press, 1956).

————, "The City in the Future of Democracy," *American Political Science Review* 61 (December 1967), pp. 953-71.

————, *Polyarchy* (New Haven: Yale University Press, 1971).

Davies, James C., "Toward a Theory of Revolution," *The American Sociological Review* 27 (February 1962), pp. 5-19.

Dawson, Richard E., and James A. Robinson, "Interparty Competition, Economic Variables and Welfare Politics in the American States," *Journal of Politics* 25 (1963), pp. 265-89.

Dubey, Sumati N., "Community Action Programs and Citizen Participation: Issues and Confusions," *Social Work* 15 (1970), pp. 76-84.

Easton, David, *The Political System: An Inquiry into the State of Political Science* (New York: Alfred A. Knopf, Inc., 1953).

————, and Robert Hess, "The Child's Political World," *Midwest Journal of Political Science* 6 (August 1962), pp. 229-46.

————, and Jack Dennis, "The Child's Acquisition of Regime Norms: Political Efficacy," *American Political Science Review* 61 (March 1967), pp. 25-38.

Eisinger, Peter K., "Protest Behavior and the Integration of Urban Political Systems," *The Journal of Politics* 33 (November 1971), pp. 980-1007.

————, "Community Control and Liberal Dilemmas," *Publius* 2 (Fall 1972), pp. 129-48.

————, "The Conditions of Protest Behavior in American Cities," *American Political Science Review* 67 (March 1973), pp. 11-29.

Elazar, Daniel J., *American Federalism: A View from the States* (New York: Thomas Y. Crowell, 1966).

English, Gary, "The Trouble with Community Action," *Public Administration Review* 32 (May/June 1972), pp. 224-32.

Erbe, William, "Social Involvement and Political Activity," *American Sociological Review* 29 (April 1964), pp. 198-215.

Fantini, Mario, Marilyn Gittell, and Richard Magat, *Community Control and the Urban School* (New York: Praeger, 1970).

Farkas, Suzanne, "The Federal Role in Urban Decentralization," *American Behavioral Scientist* 15 (September/October 1971), pp. 15-36.

Fox, Daniel M., "Federal Standards and Regulations for Participation," in *Citizen Participation: Effecting Community Change*, Edgar S. Cahn and Barry A. Passett, eds. (New York: Praeger, 1971).

Gamson, William A., *Power and Discontent* (Homewood, Illinois: The Dorsey Press, 1968).

Gilbert, Neil, *Clients or Constituents* (San Francisco: Josey-Bass, 1970).

Gordon, Robert A., "Issues in Multiple Regression," *American Journal of Sociology* 73 (1968), pp. 592-616.

Greenstein, Fred, *Children and Politics* (New Haven: Yale University Press, 1965).

Grove, Walter and Herbert Costner, "Organizing the Poor: An Evaluation of a Strategy," *Social Science Quarterly* 50 (December 1969), pp. 643-57.

Gurr, Ted, "A Causal Model of Civil Strife: A Comparative Analysis," *American Political Science Review* 62 (1968), pp. 1104-1125.

Gusfield, Joseph, "Mass Society and Extremist Politics," *American Sociological Review* 27 (February 1962), pp. 19-30.

Hallman, Howard W., *Community Corporations and Neighborhood Control* (Washington, D.C.: Center for Governmental Studies, 1970).

_____, "Federally Financed Citizen Participation," *Public Administration Review* 32 (September 1972), pp. 421-28.

Hart, David K., "Theories of Government Related to Decentralization and Citizen Participation," *Public Administration Review* 32 (October 1972), pp. 603-22.

Hawkins, Brett W., *Politics and Urban Policies* (Indianapolis: Bobbs-Merrill, 1971).

Hawley, Amos H., "Community Power and Urban Renewal Success," *American Journal of Sociology* 68 (January 1963), pp. 422-31.

Herbert, Adam W., "Management Under Conditions of Decentralization and Citizen Participation," *Public Administration Review* 32 (October 1972), pp. 622-38.

Hofstadter, Richard, *The Age of Reform* (New York: Alfred A. Knopf, 1955).

HUD News (Washington, D.C.: May 1971).

Hyman, Herbert H., *Secondary Analysis of Sample Surveys* (New York: John Wiley and Sons, 1972).

Hyneman, Charles, "Who Makes Our Laws?" *Political Science Quarterly* 55 (December 1940), pp. 556-81.

Iglitzin, Lynne B., *Violent Conflict in American Society* (San Francisco: Chandler Publishing Company, 1972).

Jacob, Herbert, and Michael Lipsky, "The Consequences of Malapportionment: A Note of Caution," *Social Forces* 43 (1964), pp. 256-61.

———, "Outputs, Structure, and Power: An Assessment of Changes in the Study of State and Local Politics," in *Political Science*, Marian D. Irish, ed. (Englewood, New Jersey: Prentice-Hall, 1968).

James, Dorothy Buckton, "The Limits of Liberal Reform," *Politics and Society* 2 (Spring 1972), pp. 301-322.

Jones, Charles O., *An Introduction to the Study of Public Policy* (Belmont, California: Duxbury Press, 1970).

Katznelson, Ira, "Antagonistic Ambiguity: Notes on Reformism and Decentralization," *Politics and Society* 3 (Spring 1972), pp. 323-33.

Kaufman, Herbert, "Administrative Decentralization and Political Power," paper presented at the meeting of the American Political Science Association, September 1968.

Kessel, John, "Government Structure and Political Environment: A Statistical Note About American Cities," *American Political Science Review* (September 1962), pp. 615-20.

Kornhauser, William, *The Politics of Mass Society* (Glencoe, Illinois: The Free Press, 1959).

Kotler, Milton, *Neighborhood Government* (Indianapolis: Bobbs-Merrill, 1969).

Kramer, Ralph, *Participation of the Poor* (Englewood Cliffs, New Jersey: Prentice-Hall, 1969).

Kramer, Daniel C.,, *Participatory Democracy: Developing Ideals of the Political Left* (Cambridge, Massachusetts: Schenkman Publishing Company, 1972).

Langton, Kenneth P., *Political Socialization* (New York: Oxford Press, 1969).

Levitan, Sar, *The Great Society's Poor Law* (Baltimore: The Johns Hopkins Press, 1969).

Liberson, Stanley, and Arnold R. Silverman, "The Precipitants and Underlying Conditions of Race Riots," *American Sociological Review* 30 (December 1965), pp. 887-98.

Lijphart, Arend, "Comparative Politics and the Comparative Model," *American Political Science Review* 65 (September 1971), pp. 682-94.

Lineberry, Robert L., and Edmund P. Fowler, "Reformism and Public Policies in American Cities," *American Political Science Review* 61 (September 1967), pp. 701-16.

———, and Ira Sharkansky, *Urban Politics and Public Policy* (New York: Harper and Row, 1971).

Lipsky, Michael, "Protest as a Political Resource," *American Political Science Review* 62 (December 1968), pp. 1144-58.

Litt, Edgar, "Jewish Ethno-Religious Involvement and Political Liberalism," *Social Forces* (May 1961), pp. 328-32.

_____ , "Ethnic Status and Political Perspectives," *Midwest Journal of Political Science* (August 1961), pp. 276-83.

Making Democracy Work (National Federation of Settlements and Neighborhood Centers: New York, 1966).

Marris, Peter, and Martin Rein, *Dilemmas of Social Reform* (Chicago: Aldine Publishing Company, 1967).

Marshall, Dale Rogers, *The Politics of Participation in Poverty* (Berkeley: University of California Press, 1971).

Matthews, Donald R., *The Social Background of Political Decision-Makers* (Garden City, New York: Doubleday and Company, 1954).

Milbrath, Lester, *Political Participation* (Chicago: Rand McNally, 1965).

Mogulof, Melvin B., *Citizen Participation: A Review and Commentary on Federal Policies and Practices* (Washington, D.C.: The Urban Institute, 1970).

Moynihan, Daniel P., *Maximum Feasible Misunderstanding* (New York: The Free Press, 1970).

Municipal Year Book, 1966 (Chicago: The International City Management Association, 1966).

National Commission on Urban Problems, *Building the American City* (Washington, D.C.: U.S. Government Printing Office, 1968).

Neal, Arthur C., and Melvin Seeman, "Organizations and Powerlessness: A Test of the Mediation Hypothesis," *American Sociological Review* 24 (April 1964), pp. 216-26.

Noell, James J., "Letter to the Editor," *American Political Science Review* 64 (December 1970), pp. 1249-51.

Pateman, Carole, *Participation and Democratic Theory* (Cambridge: Cambridge University Press, 1970).

Peterson, Paul E., "Forms of Representation: Participation of the Poor in the Community Action Program," *The American Political Science Review* 64 (June 1970), pp. 491-508.

Phillips, Bernard S., *Social Research Strategy and Tactics* (New York: The MacMillan Company, 1969).

Pitkin, Hanna, *The Concept of Representation* (Berkeley: University of California Press, 1967).

Ranney, David C., *Planning and Politics in the Metropolis* (Columbus: Merrill, 1969).

Robinson, John P., Jerrold G. Rusk, and Kendra B. Head, *Measures of Political Attitudes* (Ann Arbor, Michigan: Institute for Social Research, 1968).

Sartori, Giovanni, *Democratic Theory* (Detroit: Wayne State Press, 1962).

Schmandt, Henry J., "Municipal Decentralization: An Overview," *Public Administration Review* 32 (October 1972), pp. 571-89.

Schnore, Leo and Robert Alford, "Forms of Government and Socio-economic

Characteristics of Suburbs," *Administrative Science Quarterly* 7 (June 1963), pp. 1-17.

Schumpeter, Joseph A., *Capitalism, Socialism and Democracy* (New York: Harper and Row, 1965).

Scott, William G., "Organization Government: The Prospects for a Truly Participative System," *Public Administration Review* 32 (October 1972), pp. 622-38.

Selltiz, Claire, Marie Jahoda, Morton Deutsch, and Stuart Cook, *Research Methods in Social Relations* (New York: Holt, Rinehart and Winston, 1962).

Selover, William C., "The View from Capitol Hill," in *On Fighting Poverty: Perspectives from Experience*, James L. Sundquist and C.S. Schelling, eds. (New York: Basic Books, 1969).

Shaffer, William R., and Ronald E. Weber, "Policy Responsiveness in the American States," paper delivered at the 1972 *American Political Science Association* meeting in Washington, D.C.

_____ , "Dimensions of Political Culture in the American States," unpublished paper.

Sherbenou, Edgar, "Class, Participation, and the Council-Manager Plan," *Public Administration Review* 21 (Summer 1961), pp. 131-35.

Stein, Maurice R., *The Eclipse of Community* (Princeton: Princeton University Press, 1960).

Stenberg, Carl W., *The New Grass Roots Government?* (Washington, D.C.: Advisory Commission on Intergovernmental Relations, 1972).

_____ , "Citizens and the Administrative State: From Participation to Power," *Public Administration Review* 32 (May/June 1972), pp. 190-98.

Strange, John H., "The Impact of Citizen Participation on Public Administration," *Public Administration Review* 32 (September 1972), pp. 457-70.

Sullivan, John L., "A Note on Redistributive Politics," *American Political Science Review* 66 (December 1972), pp. 1301-1306.

Sundquist, James L., and David W. Davis, *Making Federalism Work* (Washington, D.C.: The Brookings Institution, 1969).

Sutton, Willis A., "Differential Perceptions of Impact of a Rural Anti-Poverty Campaign," *Social Science Quarterly* 50 (December 1969), pp. 657-88.

Theodore, Eustics and Carol Theodore, "Citizen Awareness and Involvement in Poverty Action," *Social Problems* 19 (Spring 1972), pp. 484-96.

U.S. Advisory Commission on Intergovernmental Relations, *Fiscal Balance in the American Federal System* (Washington, D.C.: U.S. Government Printing Office, 1967).

U.S. Congress, Senate, *Staff Study of Major Riots and Civil Disorders—1965 through July 31, 1968*, prepared by the Permanent Sub-committee on Investigations of the Committee on Government Operations, 90th Cong., 2nd sess., 1968.

U.S. National Advisory Commission on Civil Disorders, *Report of the National*

Advisory Commission on Civil Disorders (Washington, D.C.: U.S. Government Printing Office, 1968).

Urban Renewal Directory (Washington, D.C.: U.S. Department of Housing and Urban Development, December 31, 1971).

Vanceko, James J., "Community Mobilization and Institutional Change," *Social Science Quarterly* 50 (December 1969), pp. 609-631.

Van Till, Jon and Sally Van Till, "Citizen Participation in Social Policy: The End of the Cycle?" *Social Problems* 17 (1969-1970), pp. 313-23.

Walker, Jack L., "A Critique of the Elitist Theory of Democracy," *The American Political Science Review* 60 (1966), pp. 285-95.

Washnis, George J., *Neighborhood Facilities and Municipal Decentralization* (Washington, D.C.: Center for Governmental Studies, 1971).

Weber, Ronald E., and William R. Shaffer, "Public Opinion and American State Policy-Making," paper delivered at the 1970 meeting of the Midwest Political Science Association in Chicago, Illinois.

_____, and William R. Shaffer, "The Costs and Benefits of American State-Local Government Policies," paper delivered at the annual meeting of the *Southwestern Political Science Association* in San Antonio, March 30, 1972.

Wilson, James Q., and Edward C. Banfield, "Public Regardingness as a Value Premise in Voting Behavior," *American Political Science Review* 58 (December 1964), pp. 876-87.

_____, "Planning and Politics: Citizen Participation in Urban Renewal," in *Urban Renewal: People, Politics and Planning*, Jewell Bellush and Murray Hausknecht (New York: Doubleday, 1967).

Wolfinger, Raynond E., and John O. Field, "Political Ethos and the Structure of City Government," *American Political Science Review* 60 (June 1966), pp. 306-326.

Wood, Robert C., *Suburbia* (Boston: Houghton Mifflin Company, 1958).

_____, "The Contributions of Political Science to Urban Form," in *Urban Life and Form*, Werner Z. Hirsch, ed. (New York: Holt, Rinehart and Winston, 1963).

Yates, Douglas, "Neighborhood Government," *Policy Sciences* 2 (July 1972), pp. 209-219.

Zimmer, Basil, and Amos Hawley, "The Significance of Membership in Associations," *American Journal of Sociology* 65 (September 1959), pp. 196-220.

Zimmerman, Joseph F., "Neighborhoods and Citizen Involvement," paper presented at the National Conference on Public Administration, Denver, April 20, 1971.

_____, *The Federated City* (New York: St. Martin's Press, 1972).

_____, "Neighborhoods and Citizen Involvement," *Public Administration Review* 32 (May/June 1972), pp. 201-210.

Zurcher, Louis A., "The Poverty Board: Some Consequences of 'Maximum

Feasible Participation,' " *Journal of Social Issues* 26 (Summer 1970), pp. 85-107.

Indexes

Author Index

Subject Index

Advisory Commission on Intergovernmental Relations: 23, 24.
Apathy and Citizen Participation: 4–5.
Attitudinal Characteristics of Citizen Participants: 80–86.

Champaign, Illinois: 29, 33.
City Government (see Municipal Government).
City Size and Citizen Participation: 40, 42–43, 73.
City Type and Citizen Participation: 40–41, 42–43.
Citizen Participation and attitudinal characteristics: 80–86; city size, 40, 42–43, 73; city type, 40–41, 42–43; classical democratic theory, 3, 5–6; contemporary democratic theory, 3–4; cultural and ethnic influences, 35, 36–39, 73, 123–124; delivery of municipal services, 9–10, 82, 99–100, 103–106, 127; democratic theory, 3–7; demographic characteristics, 78–79, 88–95; ethnicity, 43–45, 48–51; evaluation of program success, 86–88; federal grants in aid, 62–65, 66, 73, 124–125; mayoralty strength, 27, 66, 73; method of classification, 16–20, 24–27; metropolitan fragmentation, 27, 53–54, 66; municipal politics, 65–75; municipal reformism, 27, 55–59, 66; the policy process model: 35–36, 77–78, 122; political behavior, 100–102; political efficacy, 7, 33, 128–131; political support, 11–12; political trust, 33, 99, 100–103, 106–114, 126–127; public confidence (see political trust); race, 47–48, 73; regional influences, 41, 42–43; revenue sharing, 62, 64–65, 74–75; social class, 45–47, 48–51; socialization theory, 2–3; theoretical and philosophical foundations, 2–7; the urban environment, 51–52, 66–75; urban violence and disorder, 7–9, 28, 59–62, 66, 73, 99.
Citizens' Image of Government (see political trust).

Class Influence and Citizen Participation: 45–47, 48–51, 73.
Classification Scheme of Citizen Participation Programs: 16–20, 24–27.
Coleman Report: 9.
Community Action Agency: 11, 12, 13–15, 118–119.
Community Involvement in Citizen Participation Programs: 129, 131.
Congress of Racial Equality: 10.
Consequences of Demographic Characteristics of Participants: 92–95.
Co-option and Citizen Participation Programs: 135–136.
Cultural Influences and Citizen Participation: 35, 36–39, 123–124.

Data Collection and Interviewing Procedures: 28–34.
Dayton, Ohio: 29, 31–32.
Delivery of Municipal Services and Citizen Participation: 9–10, 82, 99–100, 103–106.
Democratic Theory and Citizen Participation: 3–7, 88–89, 128–132.
Demographic Characteristics of Citizen Participants. 78–79, 88–95.
Demonstration Cities and Metropolitan Act of 1966: 14–15.
Descriptive Characteristics of Citizen Participants (see Demographic Charcteristics).

Economic Opportunity Act of 1964: 11, 12, 13–15.
Environmental Influences and Citizen Participation: 51–52, 66–75.
Ethnic Influences and Citizen Participation: 43–45, 48–51, 73, 123–124.
Evaluation of Program Success: 86–88, 113–120, 126, 127–128, 129, 134–137.

Factor Analysis of Political and Environmental Influences: 167–162.
Federal Grants in Aid and Citizen Participation: 62–65, 66, 73, 124–125.
Formal Representation: 25.

177

About the Author

Richard L. Cole received the B.A. and M.A. from North Texas State University and the Ph.D. from Purdue University where he was a member of Phi Kappa Phi, national honor society. He is currently assistant professor of political science at George Washington University where he teaches courses in urban politics, state politics, and political methodology. Professor Cole is a member of several national and regional professional organizations and has contributed to the *Midwest Journal of Political Science, Urban Affairs Quarterly, Social Science Quarterly*, and other professional journals.